INSTRUCTOR'S MANUAL TO ACCOMPANY

The International Story
An Anthology with Guidelines for Reading and Writing about Fiction

Ruth Spack
Tufts University

St. Martin's Press
New York

CAMBRIDGE
UNIVERSITY PRESS

32 Avenue of the Americas, New York NY 10013-2473, USA

Cambridge University Press is part of the University of Cambridge.

It furthers the University's mission by disseminating knowledge in the pursuit of education, learning and research at the highest international levels of excellence.

www.cambridge.org
Information on this title: www.cambridge.org/9780521657969

© Cambridge University Press 1998

First published by St. Martin's Press, Inc. 1994

A catalogue record for this publication is available from the British Library

ISBN 978-0-521-65796-9 Instructor's Manual

Cambridge University Press has no responsibility for the persistence or accuracy of URLs for external or third-party internet websites referred to in this publication, and does not guarantee that any content on such websites is, or will remain, accurate or appropriate.

CONTENTS

INTRODUCTION

The International Story has grown out of my own teaching experiences. What appears in the text is the result of years of experimenting in the classroom as I tried out new stories and new approaches. For that reason, I would not expect any teacher to use all of the material in this book in one semester. Nor would I expect teachers to use only the material in this book. I think the best approach is to experiment as I continue to do, selecting what is most effective for a particular group of students and adding other readings and assignments that enrich students' experiences in and out of the classroom.

CHAPTER COMMENTS AND SUGGESTIONS

Note: Page numbers from The International Story were not available when I was writing this manual.

PART ONE: READING FICTION

Part One presents two different ways of reading a work of fiction. Chapter 1 emphasizes affective responses; Chapter 2 emphasizes analytical responses. Of course, there will be overlap: many readers react and analyze simultaneously. Nevertheless, the chapters can be presented in progression, beginning with students' initial reactions and building on those responses to move students toward more analytical reading strategies. Alternatively, Chapter 1 can be used without Chapter 2.

CHAPTER 1. Developing Effective Reading Strategies: Understanding and Responding

The readings are of varying degrees of difficulty, depending on the story and the reader. I did not select stories according to any readability formula; rather I was drawn to stories that I found compelling.

BEFORE READING

The biographical and background information is designed to provide context and to fill in cultural/historical/political gaps. Students may incorporate it into their essays but should not allow it to limit their own approach to a story.

A FIRST READING

To develop fluency, students should try to read a story through the first time without using a dictionary. When they stop to look up every other word, they lose the meaning of the whole. One way I model this process is to read a story aloud on the first day of class, while the students follow along. Even though there might be a number of unfamiliar words, students still get the gist.

ACTIVITY: Reading a short story. Almost all of the activities in this chapter relate to Kate Chopin's "The Story of an Hour." They would work well with other stories. I find it useful to spend the first class or two working with a story so that everyone shares an understanding of how a work of literature can be approached.

SUBSEQUENT READINGS

Students should understand that it is normal and necessary to reread whole texts or parts of texts in order to understand them. I make it clear that I read in this way; and that even after reading a story many times, I often see things I had never seen before.

Establishing a Goal for Reading

Learning multiple ways of reading for different purposes gives students flexibility. Although I include suggestions, my experience has been that most students develop their own strategies.

Defining Unfamiliar Vocabulary Words

Guessing meaning from context is a reading strategy that helps speed up the reading process. It does not necessarily lead to vocabulary acquisition. If students cannot guess meaning from context, they can refer to definitions in the Glossary. Using vocabulary to interpret what they read gives them the practical means to apply what they learn.

Annotating

I show students what my book looks like--notes in the margins, phrases highlighted in yellow, passages underlined--to emphasize that this is a strategy that even experienced readers use.

KEEPING A READING LOG: EXPLORING INITIAL REACTIONS

The section on keeping a reading log is separate from the section on keeping a literary journal. I recognize that the terminology can be confusing, because one instructor's "log" is another instructor's "journal." Yet I distinguish between two ways of responding in writing because each serves a different purpose. The reading log gives students free rein to respond as they want to. The literary journal is more structured, with specific topics suggested to guide students toward purposeful interpretation.

I have students practice writing a log entry during the first week of class, after I have read a story aloud. Then they can ask questions of me, as they try to figure out just what a log entry is. Most other entries are written outside of class.

I do not always collect all of the logs, but I do respond to the log entries that I receive. With some individual students, I request that all log entries be handed in, even if the rest of the class has the option not to. This approach is not meant to be punitive but to help struggling students keep up with the reading. Students usually appreciate the extra attention that my responding to the entries gives them. Class discussions are richer if students keep a log; most do so only if it is required.

I never correct or grade the logs. I see them as learning tools for students that help them become better readers and better participants in the classroom. When students spend some time writing down their reactions before they are asked to discuss them, they have time to think through what they want to say and how they want to say it. I can then go around the room, asking students to share what they have written. After they have become used to the classroom procedure and understand that all reactions (including confusion) are welcome and are considered useful, most participate readily.

Responding to the Whole Story

There is no format to follow in a reading log. The log simply reinforces the message that students can use writing to explore their understanding of what they read.

Responding to a Particular Passage: Making Double-Entry Notes

Not all students find this technique productive--and its success can depend on the passage they choose--but it is a challenging activity and can heighten interpretive powers. It also can be a brief classroom activity that produces an exciting debate.

KEEPING A LITERARY JOURNAL: WRITING ABOUT SPECIFIC TOPICS

I ask students to write at least one literary journal entry for each story I assign. At the end of each story's discussion activities in Chapter 4, I have included a sample suggestion for a journal entry topic. Of course, students can be given several journal topics to choose from (for example, one of the other discussion activities can be used as a journal topic).

I respond in writing to all of the journal entries. I occasionally locate or correct errors, since the entries are often expanded into essays; but I focus on responding to students' ideas. I try to respond positively to the content of each entry and to expand on a point, ask a clarifying question, or raise an issue intended to challenge the student further. My comments often include a quotation from the story that, I hope, sends the student back into the text to reflect anew. If necessary, I point out discrepancies or inaccuracies. I collect the entries at the end of each class and return them at the beginning of the next class. I have used different evaluation systems for the journals over the years (for example, comments only or a point system), but I have never given grades.

Students' journal entries are used to stimulate class discussions (see page 9 of this manual for a description of the procedure).

ACTIVITY: Responding to a student journal. My own initial response to this entry was (1) that there needed to be better use of the quotation and (2) that it made sense until the second paragraph. Then I was quite surprised by C.P.'s statement that Chopin "criticizes" her main character and "punishes" her with death for wanting too much. A typical feminist reading of this story is that Chopin is sympathetic, not critical, toward Louise. I did not criticize C.P. when I commented on her journal entry, however. I have learned through experience that students' responses are valid; they

4

always make me think. It may be that Chopin does kill off her heroine for living in a fantasy world. Who can say for sure?

PARTICIPATING IN CLASS DISCUSSIONS

For a discussion of the procedure I use for class discussions, see pages 8-9 of this manual.

CHAPTER 2. Developing Effective Reading Strategies: Analyzing and Interpreting

To enhance students reading strategies, Chapter 2 introduces some terms traditionally used to analyze literature: *plot, setting, character*, and so on. (*Note:* Chapter 5 expands on these terms to help students select evidence for an interpretive essay.)

EXAMINING ELEMENTS WITHIN A STORY

These literary terms can be taught directly, but I try to design the course so that students discover them inductively. That is, in their initial responses to a story (see Chapter 1), they discuss what happened, where and when, and to whom. Only afterwards do I identify the terms *plot, setting*, and *character* (of course, some students already know the terms). I usually do so in the first week of class, so that everyone has a shared vocabulary with which to discuss a story. On the second day of class, I sometimes hand out a sheet that includes the questions they might ask to analyze the story we read on the first day of class (see the last activity in Chapter 2 or the cubing activity in Chapter 5 as examples of the questions that might be appropriate). As they answer the questions, I briefly define the terms or ask them to do so. I suggest that they read the lengthier definitions in the book at home (by listing it as a reading assignment on the syllabus).

The material in The International Story can work in different ways. For example, in the section on *plot*, students are given guidelines for summarizing a plot, then an activity to evaluate two sample plot summaries, then an activity to write their own summaries of the story. But students can do their own summaries first and then evaluate the sample summaries. Or they can do their own summaries first, compare them, and come up with their own guidelines for summarizing a plot before they evaluate the samples.

ACTIVITY: Evaluating summaries. There may be wildly different evaluations of the two sample student summaries. For example, in Summary A, some students object to the use of the quotation because question 4 asks, "Is the summary written primarily in the student's own words?" But other students emphasize the word "primarily" and find the use of the quotation acceptable. Some students find the point that Mrs. Mallard was "unable to accept reality" to be too interpretive and not appropriate for a summary. Such a comment leads to a discussion of what is appropriate. I cannot give an answer here that will satisfy everyone. What a summary contains depends on how it will ultimately be used. Just as a classroom exercise? as a complete essay assignment? as part of the introduction to an interpretive essay? The one thing about Summary A that I can say definitively is that there was no "door bell," and so the details are not accurate!

For the elements other than *plot*, I include two activities: (1) a creative writing task and (2) an oral analytical task. I cannot imagine that any instructor would have the time to assign all of the creative writing tasks, but I think just reading them and/or talking about them can be helpful for gaining insight into how and why a literary text is created. Again, students can learn inductively; for example, the term *setting* does not have to be defined before students describe their own rooms.

ACTIVITY: Analyzing character through a word. When they look up the word *keen* in the Glossary, students find these definitions: "sharp; strong; intellectually acute; acutely sensitive." As they apply these definitions, they discover that Chopin used one word cleverly to suggest many things about Louise Mallard. All of the definitions may fit; students should defend the one(s) they find most appropriate with supporting evidence from the text.

In the section on *symbolism*, I have tried to be sensitive to students' individual and cultural differences. What may act as a symbol in one person's mind or culture may not in another's.

RESEARCHING ELEMENTS OUTSIDE A STORY

I provide some brief historical, literary, and biographical information in The International Story and occasionally in the classroom, but I am interested mostly in students' interpretations of what they see in the text. Some students, however, like to consult outside sources.   Although I do not encourage this approach, I accept it--as long as students cite and document their sources.

On occasion, I have assigned students to research beyond the text, for example, to satisfy their curiosity about something related to what they have read (for example, class structure in nineteenth-century France; the African-American experience in the U.S. before the Civil Rights movement; the 1929 crash of the stock market; the missionary movement in Africa) and then to present their findings to the class members, each of whom has researched a different topic.

DISCOVERING THEMES

Students are often tempted to reduce a story's meaning to a one-sentence moral; some have been trained to do so.   I prefer to emphasize exploration of human behavior and social systems.   The discussions are richer and the essays more thoughtful if students explore themes rather than settle for a rigid lesson-in-life mode of analysis.

ACTIVITY: Discovering a theme.   By covering up the moral, students are forced back into the text to think about the behavior of the characters and to discover possible themes.   For example, they may observe that some people ignore reality or that they suffer from their superficiality or lack of foresight.   This is a different kind of insight from concluding that "you should (or should not) do this."

ACTIVITY: Analyzing themes.   Many different details may be offered to support the student themes.   For example: 1: There are at least two unexpected events: (a) the husband's death and (b) his return.   The first can be taken negatively (it is a sad event) and/or positively (it gives Louise freedom); the second can be taken positively (he is alive) and/or negatively (his return ends her freedom).   2: Louise's reaching for freedom coincides with the natural return of spring.   3: Apparently, Louise resents that her husband believed that he had "a right to impose a private will upon" her; this may be taken as evidence that the subordinate role of the wife was unacceptable to Chopin.   At the same time, the fact that Louise's husband returns at the end suggests that there were limits to a woman's freedom.   4: Since Louise does not succeed in holding on to her freedom, it may be that the parallel with the new spring life breaks down; only nature remains capable of renewing itself.   5: Once Louise dies, she is no longer anyone's possession.

PART TWO: ANTHOLOGY OF SHORT STORIES

I have separated Chapters 3 and 4 in **Part Two** of <u>The International Story</u> because I do not like reading or assigning stories that are immediately followed by questions or activities. I want students to be able to read the stories without having to follow anyone else's agenda as to how to respond.

It is possible to teach a course using these stories without having students look at the activities in Chapter 4 during class discussion time. For example, students can have their books open to the stories while the instructor looks at the discussion activities as a guide to the classroom conversation. By the same token, neither students nor instructor need to look at the activities. The class discussions can be driven by the students' own responses to the stories, including those they have recorded in reading logs and/or literary journals. Whatever approach is used, the course is most successful when students see that their ideas are valued and that multiple interpretations are possible.

CHAPTERS 3 AND 4: The Stories and Discussion Activities

I have included numerous discussion activities for each story in Chapter 4 of <u>The International Story</u>. Most of them emerged from actual class discussions. While they reflect the kinds of issues that are raised in my classroom, they of course cannot reflect exactly how or in what order students address those issues.

I usually spend one and a half (or two and a half) days on a short story. What that means is that usually we begin a new story in the middle or toward the end of a class session.

<u>Activity 1</u>: To begin the discussion of the new story, students share what they have written in their logs: their initial reactions to the story (see KEEPING A READING LOG, above). Often that is all that is needed to get the discussion going and continuing for quite a while. Sometimes questions are raised, sometimes passages are read aloud; students answer each other's questions and try to explain baffling passages to one another.

<u>Activity 2</u>: I ask students to summarize the story, so that the class has a common understanding. I assume that some students will come into the class confused, and I welcome that confusion. One student usually volunteers to retell what has happened and other students join in to render a more accurate or complete account. Sometimes students say that they do not know what happened, but as a group they almost always are able to extract the

essence of the plot. Some of the stories defy summary, however, especially when students disagree about what happens (see, for example, the discussion of "The Verb *to Kill*," on pages 49-51). This makes for an interesting debate, as different interpretations emerge.

Activity 3: Students often understand a story better if they relate the subject matter of the story to their own lives or ideas. Of course, this process has often occurred with the first two activities.

Remaining activities: The rest of the activities direct students to dig into an analysis of the text. I have tried to create activities in which questions are not asked, so that students do not think there is a "right" answer that the instructor/editor knows. Instead, students are asked to "explore" and "examine." (*Note:* Many of these activities are linked to the material in Chapter 6.) I ask questions mostly to move students along, point them in a different direction, or challenge their assumptions. When students act out scenes from the stories, they usually get up in front of the class and take the parts of the characters. Often this process itself creates debate, as students talk among themselves to decide whose line is whose or where characters should stand in relation to one another.

Suggested literary journal topic: At the end of the discussion activities, I include a suggested journal topic. Actually, this is not the last activity. Since we are often starting a new story in the middle of a class, we go through the first few activities (usually the first two or three) and then I assign a journal topic or a choice of topics. At the beginning of the next class, I begin the discussion by asking them to share what they wrote in their entries. Many of the journal questions are designed to create debate, and so the discussions are often lively and lengthy. As always, multiple interpretations are welcome.

In the next part of this manual, I discuss Chapters 3 and 4 together, summarizing and then discussing the stories one by one as they are arranged in the book. I make an effort to provide multiple interpretations of each story. Even as I do so, I understand that many other interpretations are possible.

"The Necklace" by Guy de Maupassant

Summary: Much to her dismay, a young woman in late nineteenth-century France was born into a family of clerks and is married to a clerk. Mathilde borrows a diamond necklace from a rich friend to wear to a ball but then loses it. She and her husband go into debt to pay for a replacement and for ten years work hard

9

to repay the debt. At the end of the story she discovers that the necklace was paste.

"The Necklace" is a story with a surprise ending and layers and layers of irony. The first line of the story establishes that the characters are living in a class-conscious society in which one's birth can determine one's destiny. By the end of the story, France's three major classes have been revealed: the upper class (represented by Mme. Forestier); the middle class (represented by the Loisels at the beginning); and the lower class (represented by Mme. Loisel at the end).

By the end of the first paragraph, we have some clues about the character of Mathilde Loisel, who "let herself be married to a little clerk." That she "let herself" may suggest that she is powerless or at least feels so, especially since she has no dowry. From whose perspective the clerk is "little" is open to debate. It may be Mathilde's perspective, and the word "little" may indicate her contempt toward her husband. Or it may be the perspective of the narrator, someone who sympathizes with Mathilde because she is trapped--or someone who is contemptuous of her. By the second paragraph, we learn that she is "unhappy as though she had really fallen from her proper station." This perspective seems to be that of Mathilde, who sees herself as worthy of membership in a higher class. But, again, this may be the perspective of the narrator, someone who is critical of Mathilde--or someone who understands the depth of her despair and the unfairness of the social system.

A close analysis of the third and fourth paragraphs reveals that while Mathilde "suffered ceaselessly," she does have a maid and food on the table, the "good *pot-au-feu*" that her easily satisfied husband so appreciates. Other contradictions and contrasts add to the irony of the tale. For example, in the fifth paragraph, we learn that "she had no dresses" to wear to the ball; but later her husband advises her to wear "the dress you go to the theater in." Students can discuss what Mathilde means by "no dresses" (nothing that makes her look rich, etc.). The details in the third and fourth paragraphs reveal, through her fantasies, what upper-class society looks like. Whether that society is admirable is subject to debate.

In the scene in which the Loisels discuss the ball invitation, Mathilde appears to be difficult, self-centered, and materialistic. Students usually are sympathetic to the husband. But he, too, has his own interests. He was saving for his own pleasure: "a little shooting." Students can discuss the relative value of shooting larks. Even if they find it to be a worthless venture, however, they are likely to credit him for sacrificing his own desires for hers. An irony in this scene is that Mathilde rejects the idea of wearing "natural" flowers; in the end, she wears "paste." Another irony is that she says "there's nothing more humiliating than to look poor among other women who are rich." She doesn't yet know what looking poor really means. Also, ironically, in the end, she is "proud," not humiliated, when she sees Mme. Forestier, even though she looks poor.

In the scene in which she borrows the necklace, Mme. Forestier gives her a choice of jewels. Mathilde asks to see more. It may be that at first Mme. Forestier offers her real jewels and that, ironically, in her greed, Mathilde selects a fake (this is pure speculation!).

At the ball, Mathilde has momentary success; but her life changes suddenly after she loses the necklace because she rushes out to avoid being seen in her "common" coat. Once demanding, she now follows her husband's lead, who directs her to lie to Mme. Forestier. At the jeweler's, there is a clue that there is something fishy about the necklace: the jeweler had furnished only the case, not the necklace (further evidence that things are not what they appear to be). But the Loisels purchase the real thing and suffer the consequences. Students can discuss the morality of their action. Why did they not tell the truth?

Ironically, in her effort to become a member of high-class society, Mathilde becomes a member of the lower class. Nevertheless, some students argue that her life has changed for the better. No longer a hopeless dreamer, Mathilde has become a hard-working realist. She now plays her part "with heroism." She appears to have lost her materialistic impulses as she is driven to repay the debt. As she approaches Mme. Forestier at the end, she smiles "with a joy which was proud," showing that she takes pride in her accomplishment.

Often when students write about "The Necklace" to prove that Mathilde's life has improved, however, they conveniently ignore the ending: her discovery that the necklace was a fake. If Maupassant believes she has changed for the better, why does he punish her with this discovery? And why does the author say she is "naive"? Can it be that she has done all this for nothing, without realizing it? Has her pride been a false pride? Ironically, in telling the truth to Mme. Forestier, she learns that she has paid an even higher price than she had thought in lying to her in the first place.

Because of this, some students see Mathilde's life as a disaster and the story as a morality tale: "Maupassant tries to tell us that you cannot be happy if you don't accept your station in life." In fact, one Korean student wrote that "in the view of traditional Oriental philosophy, Mme. Loisel is the typical secular type of person we should try not to be . . . . Because of her character she is necessarily destined to deserve such an avoidable and unnecessary affliction." While this interpretation makes sense and is valid from a certain perspective, I encourage students to try also to examine the complexity of the story without reducing it to a lesson in life. Here I find it useful to discuss moral versus theme (see Chapter 2). One question that gets at Maupassant's observation of human behavior and the values of the society is this: Are any of the characters worthy of emulation? Even Mme. Forestier is deceitful: she lends a fake necklace and then acts arrogantly when it is returned late. What does it mean to be a member of the upper class, then? Is that truly a superior position in society? Is any position superior?

And what might the necklace symbolize? (This would make a good literary journal question.) There are many possible answers. Duplicity. Materialism. False values. Upper-class society. The meaninglessness of life. And so on.

And what of the statement, "How little a thing is needed for us to be lost or to be saved!" What is this "little thing"? If this is Mathilde's thought, is she referring to the loss of the necklace? Does she now realize the value of her previous middle-class existence and accept her lot in life? Or has she missed the point? Is what happened really a "little" thing? Isn't it rather enormous, given the consequences? And is she "lost" or is she "saved"? Saved, if students think that her life has been changed for the better. Lost, if she has not understood the depth of the issue. None of these questions has a "right" answer.

FURTHER READING

"Guy de Maupassant." European Writers: The Romantic Century. Ed.
    Jacques Barzun. New York: Scribner's, 1985. 1759-84.
Brooks, Cleanth, and Robert P. Warren. Understanding Fiction, 3rd
    ed. Englewood Cliffs, NJ: Prentice, 1979. 72-74.
Lerner, Michael G. Maupassant. New York: Brazillier, 1975.

"A Trifle from Real Life" by Anton Chekhov

Summary: The parents of an eight-year-old boy, Aliosha, are separated; and the mother, Olga, is having an affair. Aliosha

12

confides in his mother's lover, Belayeff, that he has secretly been visiting his father. When Belayeff tells Olga the truth, despite his pledge of honor to keep the boy's secret, Aliosha is heartbroken about the betrayal.

The first paragraph of the story focuses on Nikolai Ilitch Belayeff. For an analysis of his character and the use of imagery in this paragraph, see the discussion on pages 77-78 of this manual, under "ACTIVITY: Analyzing images."

In the second paragraph, the narrator refers to Belayeff as "my hero." Students can discuss what a hero is and whether Chekhov is using the term in its literary sense and/or in another sense.

In the scene in which Aliosha tells Belayeff his secret, beginning with the third paragraph of the story, we learn that until now, Belayeff has "never cared to think" about Aliosha before. Depending on one's view, his lack of interest in a child may reveal a flaw in his character. Now, out of boredom, he focuses on Aliosha. His interest is heightened by his realization that the boy reminds him of the way Olga looked when they began their affair (described, using the book metaphor again, as "the first pages of their romance"). Perhaps he hopes that a conversation with Aliosha will pull him out of the tedium he feels. Aliosha seems to be comfortable with Belayeff, in spite of the fact that they have never shared a relationship: he runs to Belayeff when called and nestles close to him. He obviously has observed Belayeff before, noting that he has cut his beard. In his comfort, he becomes quite talkative and mentions his father. Belayeff knows how to manipulate the child. He uses the affectionate phrase "little monkey" to bring Aliosha close and repeats "Honor bright!" to assure Aliosha that he will keep the secret from Olga.

In the next part of the story, Aliosha tells Belayeff that Pelagia takes him and his sister to see his father twice a week. From his perspective, his father is warm, loving, funny, and generous (he has promised him a pony). He also believes that his father still loves his mother. From a reader's perspective, all of this might be true; but it might also be true that the father is manipulative and deceptive. He may be bribing the children with gifts, spoiling them with sweet foods, perhaps attempting to buy their love. Apparently he is encouraging the children to leave their mother when they get bigger, hardly a sign of love toward her. On the other hand, he does appear to be sincerely concerned about his wife, and he plays a proper parental role when he teaches the children to be respectful and obedient to her. Is he using the children to achieve his own ends or does he sincerely enjoy being with them? Or both?

Belayeff pumps Aliosha for information, wanting to know what the father says about him. When he learns that the father blames him for the family's misfortune, he becomes angry. He seems to find irony in the idea that everyone assumes that he is "frightfully happy." At that moment, Olga comes home and is confronted with an excited Belayeff. His hollow values are revealed when he indicates that his needs are "more important than words of honor." Ironically, this hypocritical liar is concerned about the father's "hypocrisy" and intolerable "lies." Although Olga is witness to Aliosha's pain, she leaves the room. Apparently, she is more concerned about finding out if she has been betrayed than she is about her son's emotional needs. Her concern about being betrayed seems hypocritical if, in fact, Belayeff is right when he says that the father is the "injured" party in this affair.

At the end, Belayeff, too, ignores Aliosha. The boy can turn only to his little sister to tell her "how he had been deceived." The narrator tells us that this is "the first time in his life that he had come roughly face to face with deceit." This statement is worthy of examination. Is it really the first time? Hasn't his father been deceitful in seeing the children behind his wife's back? Hasn't Pelagia been deceitful in bringing the children to their father without Olga's knowledge? Hasn't Aliosha himself been deceitful? Does this mean, then, that this is not only the first time he is aware of adult deceit but also the first time he confronts his own? That he had never before imagined "things for which no name could be found in the vocabulary of childhood" suggests that he has now left his innocence behind and entered the cynical world of adulthood. His sad behavior at the end contrasts sharply with his carefree behavior at the beginning of the story. His "restless little body" and his upper-class status--signaled by his velvet suit--cannot protect him from becoming the "martyr" that he is foreshadowed to be.

FURTHER READING

Kramer, Karl D. The Chameleon and the Dream: The Image of Reality in Chekhov's Stories. The Hague: Mouton, 1970.
Matlaw, Ralph E. Anton Chekhov's Short Stories: Texts of the Stories, Backgrounds, Criticism. New York: Norton, 1979.
Rayfield, Donald. Chekhov: The Evolution of His Art. New York: Barnes, 1975. 197-200.

"Two Portraits" by Kate Chopin

Summary: "Two Portraits" tells two stories of a woman named Alberta. In the first story, Alberta is a beautiful, seductive wanton who is aging and becoming alcoholic. In the second story Alberta is a beatific, devoted nun who is the most saintly woman in the convent.

Chopin begins each portrait with the same paragraph. The first line, "Alberta not having looked very long into life," suggests that neither Alberta is yet an adult; the second, "had not looked very far," suggests that neither has had broad exposure. That each Alberta "put out her hands to touch things that pleased her" emphasizes the physical, sensual way in which she experiences life. That each was "drinking impressions and treasuring them in her soul" emphasizes her sensory and deeply felt approach to life. Each Alberta, too, radiates love. How ironic that both a wanton and a nun can be described in this way. How can this be?

One interpretation is that Chopin shows how a different environment and upbringing can determine a person's future. In the first part, "The Wanton," Alberta is raised in what can be described only as a cycle of abuse. She is regularly beaten and then given gifts by the woman who brings her up, someone who is unstable and incapable of providing proper parental guidance. This woman allows artists to paint young Alberta naked. Desperate for affection, Alberta looks forward to her sessions with her tutor, who fondles her. After her "mama" apparently commits suicide, Alberta, abandoned by everyone she has known, is taken in by a kindly couple. But it seems that they groom her for prostitution, and by age seventeen she is in business. As Alberta gets older, she lives in fear of the aging process but consoles herself with the possibility of suicide; she lives only for the pleasure of the moment. The difficult circumstances of her childhood have hardened her. Her increasing use of alcohol makes her ill-tempered and even potentially violent.

In the second part, "The Nun," Alberta is guided by a "holy woman" who introduces her to the beauty of nature and to the supremacy of God's love. Unlike the first Alberta, who gives in to outward temptation to achieve earthly pleasure, this Alberta turns inward. At the age when other women are aroused by physical love, she knows only spiritual love. Disturbed by the material world, she enters a convent. She uses her external senses to perceive elements of the spiritual world: "Her ears seem to hear sounds that reach no other ears; and what her eyes see, only God and herself know." Unlike the wanton, who uses her beauty to

1 5

seduce, the nun is unaware of her beauty, which is illumined by her devotion. Both Albertas give love. But the first receives none in return and is unable to find inner peace, while the second is loved by God and finds ecstasy in prayer and in visions. Both are physical in their actions, with different results: the first uses her body to please men, while the second heals others through her touch. Unlike the wanton, who would die early to protect her beauty, the nun would die for Christ.

While it may be that Chopin shows that one's upbringing determines one's destiny, another interpretation of the story might be that the two portraits represent two sides of human nature, for example, wicked/good or body/soul. Perhaps Chopin examines the struggle of opposites--the two Albertas--in each of us.

Another interpretation may be that while the nun in society appears to be different from the wanton, in essence she is similar. In both portraits, for example, the women are passionate. Perhaps the nun's emotional state is merely a sublimation of or substitution for her physical desires. (It might also be possible, but difficult given her aging process, to defend the argument that the first Alberta mends her ways and becomes a nun.)

Yet another interpretation could be that Chopin is commenting on the limited roles of women in nineteenth-century society. To some students, neither of the portraits is admirable. Are Alberta's only options, if she chooses not to marry, to be either a wanton or a nun? One choice makes her a pariah in society and puts her at risk. The other isolates her from society and deprives her of control over her life.

FURTHER READING

Kennelly, Karen, ed. American Catholic Women: A Historical Exploration, New York: Macmillan, 1989.
Seyersted, Per. Kate Chopin: A Critical Biography. Baton Rouge: Louisiana State U P, 1969.
Toth, Emily. Kate Chopin, New York: Morrow, 1990.

"The Americanization of Shadrach Cohen" by Bruno Lessing

Summary: A nineteenth-century Russian Jewish immigrant joins his sons in New York. Embarrassed by his old-fashioned and religious appearance and demeanor, the sons try to change him into a "progressive" American man. One day, angered by the fact that they are ashamed of him, Shadrach declares that he will become Americanized. He takes over their business and demands that they obey him and follow their religion strictly. The sons become more respectful and disciplined, and the father adapts to America.

The two sons are described as rather well-to-do, modern, and stylish: each wears a diamond and both are "dapper-looking." However, their neckties are "flaring," suggesting that their attire may be a bit loud and ostentatious. (Perhaps the other meaning of "flaring"--angry--suggests something about their temperaments.) Proud of their own Americanized appearance, they are appalled that their father is the stereotypical immigrant. Given that they haven't seen him for five years, the fact that the first thing they want to do is to take him to a barbershop reflects their hollow values. They treat Marta, the serving-woman, as an object, disrespectful of her role as the woman who nursed their mother until she died. Selfish and materialistic, they tolerate their father only because they want his money.

Shadrach, on the other hand, reacts with dignity. He retains his Russian Jewish identity, remains loyal to Marta, generously offers money to his sons, and initially does not lose his temper. Eventually, however, he loses patience when Gottlieb refuses to introduce him to his American fiancee. In a humorous turn, he declares that he will become Americanized and immediately treats Gottlieb like a child, sending him to bed.

There can be at least two interpretations of Shadrach's character. One view of his behavior is that, although the story has a happy ending, the end does not justify the means. First, Shadrach's initial refusal to adapt in any way to an American way of life is obstinate. Immigrants should be willing to accept changes; after all, coming to the United States means starting a new life. Secondly, his sudden decision to become Americanized leads him to exhibit authoritarian and undemocratic behavior: he takes total control of the business and deprives his sons of any say. He fires a rude clerk without giving him a second chance. He should have no more right to impose his way of life on his sons than they do to impose theirs on him. This interpretation suits students who believe that "Americanization" means accepting everything American, including the notion that all people are created equal and have a right to liberty and the pursuit of happiness. To students who come to this conclusion, the overall tone of the story may be solemn or even depressing, despite some humorous flashes.

Another interpretation might be that in becoming an American, Shadrach does not lose the positive values of his native culture.

Furthermore, he takes from the American world its best values: "he became broader-minded, more tolerant, and, above all, more flexible in his tenets." In addition, he influences his sons to accept the teachings of their culture: honor toward their father and respect toward their religion. This conclusion fulfills many students' definition of "Americanization": accepting the advantages and positive values of American culture while at the same time bringing the best of another culture to America. To students who come to this conclusion, the tone of the story is most likely humorous and reassuring.

FURTHER READING

Frankel, Ellen, and Betsy Platkin Teutsch, eds. The Encyclopedia of Jewish Symbols. Northvale, NJ: Aronson, 1992.
Liptzin, Sol. "The New Immigration." The Jew in American Literature. New York: Bloch, 1966. 100-22.
Walden, Daniel, ed. Introduction. On Being Jewish: American Jewish Writers from Cahan to Bellow. New York: Fawcett, 1974. 11-29.

"Araby" by James Joyce

Summary: Told by an adult narrator looking back on his childhood, "Araby" is the story of a boy who falls in love with his friend's older sister, whom he adores with religious passion. Having promised to bring her something from a bazaar named Araby, he takes a train to what he fantasizes will be an enchanted place, but he arrives just as the stalls are closing. Observing the silence, the darkness, and the discouraging behavior of the few people left in the bazaar, he loses interest in his quest.

(*Note*: I find that it is best to go through this complex story slowly in class, even paragraph by paragraph, as much of its meaning is revealed through an analysis of its images. Students may need more guidance with "Araby" than with other stories.)

Throughout the story, the details are provided by the adult narrator, whose careful use of language reveals underlying meanings that the boy could not have understood as he lived through the events. The first line of the story sets the stage for the events. The boy apparently attends the Christian Brothers' School and, with his friends, playfully makes the quiet street noisy when school is over. But the adult narrator sees the school as a place of confinement, where the boy is almost imprisoned, until he is

18

"set . . . free." Furthermore, he is freed into a dead-end ("blind") street, which suggests the limitations of life in Dublin, a place with no exit, no hope. (For a fuller discussion of this line, see page 78 of this manual, under "Symbolism.") The narrow lives of the people in this neighborhood are personified in the houses, which are "decent" (respectable; conformist) and "imperturbable" (not easily disturbed), but "detached" (isolated from one another). We soon learn that this respectable, calm exterior covers a somewhat disturbing, disordered interior.

The boy's house had once been occupied by a priest, who died there: a rather haunting image. The priest's life is linked to "waste" and "useless" contents. The innocent boy is attracted to the external: the color of the pages of one of the priest's books; but the adult narrator knows that, inside, the books are not what they appear to be or should be. *The Abbot,* suggesting a religious topic, is actually a romance; *The Memoirs of Vidocq* is a sexually suggestive book, which calls into question the priest's morality. The grounds of the house suggest the temptations of the Garden of Eden ("the wild garden") with its "central apple-tree," which was the source of Adam and Eve's disobedience to God and their subsequent acquisition of carnal knowledge. Psychoanalytic critics may find much to interpret in the phallic "rusty bicycle-pump" that apparently belonged to the priest. That the priest was "charitable" is, of course, a good quality. That someone who made a vow of poverty has so much money that he can donate to numerous institutions, however, may call into question his integrity. All in all, these details can focus readers on the differences between what a priest is expected to be--a holy man--and what this priest was really like. And the boy's life is intimately connected to this priest.

On page 77 in this manual, I discuss some of the imagery of the third paragraph. There is little light in this dark outdoor scene, except for the "feeble" lanterns. The strong light comes from the kitchen window, with Mangan's sister's "figure defined by the light from the half-opened door." What is the significance of this detail? What kind of figure is defined by light? Students may think of the Madonna or an angel, especially if they are familiar with Christian art. Therefore, Mangan's sister is a holy figure to the boy. But this figure is standing in a "half-opened door." What kind of female figure defined by light stands in a half-opened door? Students who know of red light districts may answer: a prostitute. What is Joyce suggesting? That the female is at once a Madonna and a prostitute, simultaneously a symbol of purity and of seduction? Or perhaps that to the child she is the first, and to the adult she is the latter?

19

(In either case, these are limited notions of the female provided by a male author through a male narrator.) Her presence seems to act as the transition between the boy's childish play and his awareness of sexuality: he notes that "her dress swung as she moved her body." This observation signals his adolescent development.

In the fourth paragraph, we see that the boy is serious about the girl; the adult narrator sees his behavior as "foolish." Again the word *blind* plays a role. Here it is the noun form, literally meaning a window shade, figuratively suggesting that the boy is blind to reality and/or that he creates a barrier between himself and the truth.

In the fifth paragraph, we see part of the larger environment that influences his upbringing: the marketplace in Dublin. The images are all negative: drunkenness, curses, troubles. Yet the boy is oblivious to the scene because thoughts of the girl fill his mind. In fact, the narrator uses the language of romantic fiction (shades of Sir Walter Scott) to describe the boy's vision: "I imagined that I bore my chalice safely through the throng of foes." Here, too, his love is connected with religion, suggesting the boy is on a chivalrous quest similar to the quest for the Holy Grail. Hints of his religious devotion to the girl are seen in phrases like "prayers and praises" and in his reference to a harp (heaven's instrument). The boy's Christian background has influenced his attitude toward love.

In the next paragraph, his love becomes almost obsessive. In the room where the priest died, he is "thankful that I could see so little." Literally, he is in the dark, with only a lamp or lighted window below. Figuratively, he is in the dark, unaware of the foolishness of his behavior. Again, his devotion is religious: he "pressed the palms" of his hands together as if in prayer as he reaches a state of ecstasy, repeating "O love!" over and over.

"At last she spoke to me." This is his next line, and it is interesting to discuss whether in fact she did speak to him or whether he is still in that back room, now having a religious vision. In either case, the word *Araby* (with its exotic connotation) is introduced and, since Mangan's sister is unable to go to the bazaar, he promises to bring her something. In this scene, there is a juxtaposition between sexuality and child's play. As she speaks to him, she seductively "turned a silver bracelet round and round her wrist." She is holding onto a spike of the railings (a phallic symbol?). The boy is aware of "the white curve of her neck," which is lit by the door lamp. He also can see a hint of her petticoat. At the same time, his friends are "fighting for their caps." The boy stands at the crossroads between his childhood and his adulthood.

20

Emotionally and sexually aroused, he is unable to sleep. Her image and the word *Araby* converge so that he links her with "Eastern enchantment." Perhaps still unaware of his physical attraction, he sees a spiritual connection: "my soul luxuriated." Schoolwork is now linked to childhood; he desires something more.

He gets some resistance from his aunt and uncle: from the aunt because she fears the bazaar may be anti-Catholic, from the uncle because he is too distracted. Feeling that he is treated "pitilessly," he finds comfort, paradoxically, in the "high cold empty gloomy" rooms of his house. As he waits for his uncle's return, he sees his friends below in the street; their sounds are now "weakened and indistinct," as he is moving further away emotionally from their childish interests.

In his home, as he waits, materialistic images mix with religious ones. His aunt's friend, Mrs. Mercer (mercenary?), the widow of a pawnbroker (money lender), collects stamps for some "pious" reason. No matter where the boy is, there is tension between values, a gap between appearance and reality. When his uncle finally arrives, the boy "could interpret" the uncle's behavior. Given that the uncle is "talking to himself" and that his overcoat is heavy, it may be that he is drunk, an alcoholic with liquor bottles in his pockets. He has forgotten his promise to give the boy money to go to the bazaar. At the mention of *Araby,* the uncle begins to recite *The Arab's Farewell to His Steed,* literally a popular poem, symbolically a foreshadowing of the boy's farewell to his childhood.

The scene in the train is a foreshadowing as well. The train is "deserted" and "bare," and the boy is alone in "third-class," signaling his isolation and low status in an empty world. The route to enchantment is far from enchanting: the delay is "intolerable," the train "crept," the houses are "ruinous," no one but the boy seems to be interested in going to *Araby*. The platform at the destination is "improvised," suggesting the temporal nature of enchantment, of love.

The boy finds no sixpenny entrance at the bazaar and must pay a shilling, which suggests that this is no place for a child and that he must enter this world as an adult. Expecting something "magical," the boy instead finds a "weary-looking" person, mostly "closed" stalls, "darkness," and "silence." In this place that reminds him of a "church after a service," he sees men "counting money"; again religious and materialistic images are mixed. (Those who know the New Testament may be reminded of Christ and the money changers in the church.)

The few people who are left have "English accents," suggesting privilege and power to the Irish mind. The conversation between a young "lady" and two young "gentlemen" sounds neither ladylike nor gentlemanly, nor like the dialogue of a romantic novel, nor like a reflection of a sacred relationship. Rather, it is flirtatious and centers on a "fib," again a hint at deception, the difference between truth and reality. Unlike his love's, the voice of this female is "not encouraging," and the boy reacts "humbly," reduced by her tone and attitude.

At the end of the story, the boy's trip to the bazaar is as "useless" as the papers in the waste room of his house. What little light had been there is "out"; it is now "completely dark." Paradoxically, in this darkness the boy finally sees; he is no longer blind to the fact that he has been "driven . . . by vanity," and he is now "derided" by this self-delusion and empty vision. His humiliation makes him anguished and angry. What has he realized? There are many possible answers. His love for Mangan's sister has been an illusion; she is not a Madonna, but just a simple "brown" girl. His love for religion, too, has been an illusion; the church/priest are not pure, but are tainted by materialism and immorality. His ideal of love has been shattered; love for the opposite sex involves sexual arousal: his senses cannot permanently "veil themselves." At this moment of realization, he leaves his childhood behind and emotionally enters the adult world, one in which he must confront reality. The pure, innocent, and sensitive boy begins the transformation into the sophisticated, knowledgeable, and cynical yet still sensitive adult (narrator) he will become.

FURTHER READING

Garrison, Joseph M.   "The Adult Consciousness of the Narrator in Joyce's 'Araby.'" Studies in Short Fiction 10 (1973): 416-19.
Gifford, Don. Joyce Annotated. Berkeley: U of California P, 1982. 40-48.
Stone, Harry. "'Araby' and the Writings of James Joyce." Antioch Review 25 (1965): 375-410.

"War" by Luigi Pirandello

Summary: A group of people on a train from Rome during World War I discuss what it means to be the parents of sons who fight in the war. One man insists that his son was a hero and happily died for his country, but he breaks down when questioned by a woman whose son has just been ordered to the front.

The story takes place in an "old-fashioned" train at dawn, perhaps a hint that old ways of thinking are about to see a new light. (Note: The original title of the story is "Quando si comprende," which means, "When will we understand?") The environment is less than ideal: it is "stuffy," "smoky," and "second-class." The couple who enter the train bring with them a depressing air: she is in "deep mourning" and he is "death-white." Nevertheless, the passengers create a friendly atmosphere: they are kind in finding a space for the woman, and her husband is polite in thanking them.

The woman's pain at learning that her son unexpectedly will be sent to the front makes her almost subhuman. She is a large woman reduced to a "shapeless bundle," and she has so little control over her body that she must be "hoisted in" like an object. Her movements are "twisting and wriggling" and she moans "like a wild animal." Part of her distress comes from her awareness that she will get little sympathy since everyone is involved intimately with the war.

The passengers begin their discussion with some one-upmanship and engage in a verbal battle about who is suffering most. The one whose son has just been called up? the one whose son has been serving since the first day and has been wounded twice? the one who has two sons and three nephews at the front? Given that the couple has only one son, the conversation shifts to address what it means to lose a child. How is parental love divided? Does the one with two sons suffer doubly? That discussion leads them to examine why they have children in the first place. For their own benefit? for their country? And whom do they love more, their children or their country? And whom do the draft age males love more, their country or their parents? Here the emphasis is on "decent" boys, and students can discuss what the fat traveler means by "decent." Respectable? conforming to recognized standards? obliging? well-bred? middle class? patriotic?

The fat traveler defends the death of young soldiers by claiming that someone "must go to defend the country." Is that true? To justify the death of his own son, he talks about the "illusions" of youth and remarks that to die young is to avoid "the bitterness of disillusion." Based on a message he received from his son before he died, he goes so far as to say that he died "satisfied." Is this true? Or is this just an "illusion" of youth? Or might it actually be the father's illusion? Or might the "decent" son just be playing his role to spare his father more grief? That he breaks down in tears when asked by the woman who wants to believe in his view of heroism and patriotism, "is your son really dead?" suggests that his illusion is suddenly shattered, that he recognizes the truth.

There are early hints that the fat traveler's emotions are at war. He is "panting," his eyes are "bulging," and there is evidence of "inner violence" and of something "uncontrolled." His body is "weakened," two of his teeth are "missing," his lip is "livid" (discolored? pale? angry?) and "trembling." His eyes are "motionless" and he is "shrill." The other travelers are impressed by his monologue; but clearly his words and his body do not match, until he recognizes the "inner violence" that has been wrought and what he is really "missing." Are parents as victimized as soldiers by war? What are loyalty, patriotism, and honor in the face of parental love and family values?

Like "War," the poem by Wilfred Owen is a reaction to the unquestioning patriotism of the civilian population during World War I. Unlike the story, it includes graphic details of what actually happens in battle. The soldiers, though young, are "bent" over like "old beggars." Thought of as heroic at home, at the front they are humbled by their experience. Romantically idealized by civilians as handsome, strapping men, in reality they suffer horribly from fatigue, disease, and poison gas. Far from being sweet and fitting, being at war is "bitter" and "desperate."

Is the message honorable or cowardly? Are there things worth dying for? Should soldiers be glorified?

FURTHER READING

Brooks, Cleanth, and Robert Penn Warren. Understanding Fiction.
    3rd ed. Englewood Cliffs, NJ: Prentice, 1979. 77-79.
DiYanni, Robert. Literature: Reading Fiction, Poetry, Drama, and the
    Essay. 2nd. ed. New York: McGraw, 1990. 88-89.
Giudice, Gaspare. "Politics and War." Pirandello: A Biography.
    London: Oxford U P, 1975. 69-102.

"The Egg" by Sherwood Anderson

Summary: Told by an adult narrator looking back on his childhood, "The Egg" is the story of a boy whose early days were spent on his family's chicken farm. After the family's endeavor fails, they enter the restaurant business in a different town. In an attempt to be successful, the boy's father decides to entertain his customers. But an egg trick fails to achieve its goal, and the father breaks down in tears.

The first sentence hints that the father has not turned out as nature intended. Before he married, he had a steady job, friends with whom to drink and sing, and satisfaction with his lot. He did not become ambitious until he married and had a child. His educated wife dreams that her son will grow up to be the president of the United States. Her models are Garfield and Lincoln who "rose from poverty to fame," but whom she probably does not identify as victims of assassination. The narrator, however, "a gloomy man," recognizes that dreams are often cut short by tragedy.

The narrator believes that his mother may have been the catalyst for the family's tragic ventures. Her dream is viewed almost as a sickness: she was "incurably" ambitious. Growing up on a chicken farm and watching the inevitable cycle of birth and death made the narrator "inclined to see the darker side of life." At the same time, he is capable of retelling the story with humor: "One hopes for so much from a chicken and is so dreadfully disillusioned." He sees parallels between chicken and human life (page 79 of this manual for a discussion of the chicken symbol). Those who read the literature on how to raise chickens have their hopes falsely raised. This literature is not for the inexperienced. People are more likely to find gold in Alaska or honesty in a politician than they are to succeed at chicken farming. Having been burned by experience, the narrator's approach to life, if laced with humor, is cynical.

The struggle to raise chickens is replaced by the struggle to succeed in the restaurant business: the cycle of birth/death/birth or success/failure/success repeats itself. Again, the idea was born in the mother's mind, and she herself rents the building near a town in the hope that her son will be educated there and "rise in the world." The boy dreams of a "happy eggless" life, but the egg/chicken cycle follows the family. After extraordinarily hard work, his father decides to become successful by adopting "a cheerful outlook on life" (one that he apparently lost when he got married) and entertaining his customers. He plans to do egg tricks, and the narrator notes that there was "something pre-natal about the way eggs kept themselves connected with the development of his idea." His first effort fails, but only because his customer is not looking when he succeeds in making the egg stand on end. His second effort fails when his struggle to fit an egg through a bottle neck ends in the egg breaking and spurting over his clothes (Psychoanalytic critics might see sexual humiliation here; the word *consummated* is used in the paragraph). In anger, he throws one egg and then takes another upstairs to his wife and child. Instead of destroying this egg, however, he lays it "gently" on the table. Why? Perhaps, in the presence of his son, he sees this egg as a sign of hope. If there is an egg (child/dream), there can a chicken (adult/success); the dream does not have to die.

Another, less optimistic, interpretation of the story is that the father recognizes that he cannot control the egg. He cannot destroy it because to destroy it would be to be free and he cannot be free. He is trapped in an eternal repetition: the cycle of birth/death; dream/disillusionment; hope/despair; ambition/loss of faith; parent/child; childhood/adulthood; illusion/reality; optimism/pessimism, and so on. (All of these categories, separately or together, represent what the egg might symbolize.)

How, then, does Christopher Columbus fit into this story? The father calls Columbus a "cheat" because to make an egg stand on end, he simply broke it and stood it on the broken part. The father thinks that Columbus took a short cut. But in American myth, Columbus represents the first of all great success stories: he discovered the New World. Through determination, ingenuity, and creativity, he paved the way for others to follow. Uniqueness is the secret to success. Columbus was an original, but the father is simply an imitator. Providing double irony, however, Columbus's story (like Garfield's and Lincoln's), has its darker side, as the narrator may or may not know. Columbus's success was built on the destruction of other peoples and cultures. (Of course, this view was not current in Anderson's time.)

FURTHER READING

Gerhard, Joseph. "The American Triumph of the Egg: Anderson's 'The Egg' and Fitzgerald's The Great Gatsby." Criticism 7 (1965): 131-40.
"Sherwood Anderson." American Writers. Vol. 1. New York: Scribner's, 1974.
West, Michael D. "Sherwood Anderson's Triumph: 'The Egg.'" American Quarterly 20 (1968): 675-93.

"Babylon Revisited" by F. Scott Fitzgerald

Summary: An American man returns to Paris to regain custody of the daughter he lost. After years of drinking and spending, Charlie Wales is getting his life under control. But the intrusion of two drunk friends from his past revives his sister-in-law's distrust and keeps him from getting his daughter back.

The story opens in a bar. Charlie is back in Paris, which has changed drastically: the city is "empty"; the Ritz bar is "not . . . American" anymore; he feels a "stillness," hears a "bored" voice, and encounters "only a single pair of eyes." Charlie is asking the bartender about old friends from a year and a half before and leaves his brother-in-law's address for Mr. Schaeffer. This action, we will learn, is his undoing.

In the first couple of pages, we learn that Charlie is thirty-five, that he has a daughter in Paris (a surprise to the bartender), that he's in business in Prague, that he's "going slow" in his drinking, that he had lived the high life in Paris but shows some regret about it ("He had never eaten at a really cheap restaurant . . . . [H]e wished that he had"), and that he has suffered great loss ("everything was gone").

In contrast to the bar and the city, the home of his in-laws is "warm and comfortably American" and radiates "cheer." The children interact "intimately." But the relationship between Charlie and Marion reflects opposite emotions: "From the first, there had been an instinctive antipathy between them." He feels "a cramping sensation" and cannot relax, while she is "tepid" and expresses "unalterable distrust" toward him.

Marion has lost the bloom of youth and has "worried eyes." Bitter, she cannot resist mentioning her suffering or attacking Charlie for his profligate ways. Her demeanor is marked by "coldness" and "aggressiveness." Yet her comfortable home and happy, well-mannered children suggest that she is a responsible and good mother.

Desiring custody of Honoria, Charlie must prove to Marion that he has changed. She is looking for evidence that he has not. From her perspective, he should not be in bars at all: "I should think you'd have had enough" of them. She challenges him when she learns he takes only one drink a day: "I hope you keep to it"; and she questions his ability to do so: "How long are you going to say sober, Charlie?" Even his language causes her to be critical: "Please don't swear at me," she says when he claims he's "behaving damn well." When he argues that he can give Honoria "certain advantages" like a French governess and a new apartment, Marion just sees that as evidence that he is as materialistic as ever: "I suppose you can give her more luxuries than we can." She assumes that he will start "throwing away money again." Even Lincoln has a restive look when Charlie boasts of his large income. Although she agrees to let

2 7

him take Honoria, Marion's distrust of Charlie makes her decide to retain legal guardianship for another year. When drunken Lorraine Quarrles and Duncan Schaeffer show up (an event for which Charlie is responsible, having left the Peters' address for Duncan), Marion feels vindicated and decides to keep Honoria.

From a perspective other than Marion's, has Charlie changed? As far as the drinking is concerned, students may argue that someone with a drinking problem so severe that he required rest in a sanitarium should never drink, even only once a day. (This perspective is based on current knowledge about alcoholism). Certainly, given that he is trying to get custody of his daughter, he should be careful to stay away from bars; yet at the beginning and at the end of the story, that is where he is. And perhaps he should not have agreed to have a drink at the Empire with Duncan and Lorraine in the presence of his daughter.

Charlie's desire for Honoria may be self-centered. He wants "only the tangible, visible child" perhaps more for himself than for her; he's afraid to wait any longer and lose "my chance for a home." Furthermore, he senses that he is aging and is afraid of being alone: "He wasn't young any more, with a lot of nice thoughts and dreams to have by himself."

Charlie's attitude toward money leaves something to be desired as well and is pathetic. He uses it for convenience, to pay off a woman who gives him an "encouraging stare." He also uses it to reestablish his relationship with his daughter and to purchase her love: "First, we're going to that toy store and buy you anything you like." Even his daughter has better values than that: "not the toy store . . . . I've got lots of things." Later, he buys "presents for all the Peters." In doing so, he ignores the fact that Marion resents his new wealth. Although Lincoln and Marion are proud, Charlie thinks about doing "something to get Lincoln out of his rut at the bank."

As far as his attitude toward his past, that, too, is questionable. Even though his wife has died and he has been institutionalized, he still says "it was nice while it lasted." In fact, he thinks of himself and the other drunks as "a sort of royalty, almost infallible." He seems to be in some sort of denial. Realizing that his resentment toward Marion is showing, he "modulated" his behavior to adopt the "chastened attitude of the reformed sinner." Is his change sincere or just an act?

All of these details notwithstanding, students can find much evidence that Charlie has changed. First, his drinking. When offered a cocktail by Lincoln at the beginning, he refuses, having already had his one drink. At the end, too, he turns down a second offer at the bar. When he sees the activity on the Place Blanche, he withdraws, realizing "You have to be damn drunk." In fact, his drinking problem had lasted only about a year and a half; he has been treated for it; and he has been free of it for a year and a half. Even Marion recognizes at one point that he has "arrived at control."

There is evidence, too, that Charlie will be a good father. Understanding what constitutes a meaningful relationship, he reaches out for "a new tolerance; he must be both parents to her and not shut any of her out of communication." He loves Honoria but is aware of the limitations of that love, "the injury that a father can do to a daughter . . . by attaching . . . too closely." He does not want her to forget her mother. He chooses her governess with care.

Even his attitude toward money is different. When he is denied custody, his first impulse is to use money to stay connected with Honoria: "There wasn't much he could do now except send Honoria some things." But then, he realizes that "this was just money," implying that he must find other ways to show his love.

His attitude toward his past is poignant. He understands that the "catering to vice and waste" was "childish" and that he had paid an enormous price for his actions. He drank to avoid remembering, but now he remembers "his child taken from his control, his wife escaped to a grave"; and he is haunted by these images. His new awareness changes even his past sexual behavior. He turns away a woman at a *brasserie*; and although he feels Lorraine's "passionate, provocative attraction," he does not respond to her. Even Marion at one point recognizes that Charlie is different: she saw that "his feet were planted on the earth now." His values have changed: "he believed in character." When Duncan and Lorraine arrive at the apartment, they are like "ghosts from the past." The "memory of those days swept over him like a nightmare" and he hopes that "they couldn't make him pay forever."

That line can be turned into a question: Can they make him pay forever? Can a person ever escape the past?

FURTHER READING

Fitzgerald, F. Scott. "Echoes of the Jazz Age." The Crack-Up. Ed. Edmund Wilson. New York: New Directions, 1964. 13-22.
Gross, Seymour L. "Fitzgerald's 'Babylon Revisited.'" College English 25 (1963): 128-3.
Male, Roy R. "'Babylon Revisited': The Story of the Exile's Return." Studies in Short Fiction 2 (1965): 270-77.

"The Man Who Was Almost a Man" by Richard Wright

Summary: A seventeen-year-old African American works on a farm owned by a white man.   To prove his manhood, Dave buys a gun.   He accidentally shoots his employer's mule, tries to cover up the truth, and becomes the laughing stock of the farm.   When he is told he must work for two years to pay off the debt, Dave jumps on a train heading north.

(Note: Although the dialect is daunting, when students act out the various parts, they can capture its rhythm and understand it better.   Students may complain about the language of the story at the beginning, but, like most readers, they will probably find it to be deeply affecting.)

The story is set in the South, probably in the late 1920s or early 1930s and opens on the fields.   Dave's early reference to the other workers as "niggers" brings the issue of race into the story immediately.   Dave is clearly aware of who is black and who is white.   Yet this is not a story only about relationships between races but also within them.   For Dave is not treated as he wishes to be, even by those of his own race: they "talk to him as though he were a little boy."   Among the others who deprive Dave of his manhood are his mother, who still controls his paycheck.   In his effort to show that he is a man, Dave, when alone, walks with strength: he "struck out across the fields."   He believes that a gun will change the way others treat him.

Dave is "confident" until he reaches Joe's store.   When he sees Joe's "white face," he loses his courage.   Joe's "greasy" appearance may also affect Dave's reaction; he's in the presence of a slimy personality.   Joe is the first of many in the story who laugh at Dave and yet another who calls him a "boy."   (Students can discuss the historical significance of a white man's calling a black man "boy.")   That Dave agrees to buy a gun from this man suggests his naiveté or stupidity.   He ignores important clues such as that the gun is "kinda old" and that it is a "left-hand" one.   (In a later scene, we learn that Dave is right-handed, when, after shooting, "he thought his right hand was torn from his arm.")

At first, Dave's relationship with his mother may seem problematic.   She's demanding ("Yuh git up from there and git to the well"); she's insulting ("Ah ain feedin no hogs"); and she is rough ("She grabbed his shoulder and pushed him").   Any of these details, however, might be viewed as humorous or affectionate, depending upon one's perspective.   To his mother, Dave is a "boy"; and at the

30

very least he does act like an awkward adolescent: he "stumbled," "groped," "fumbled," and "bumped."

Dave's attitude toward his father is characterized by "guilt" that he is not behaving properly. He recognizes that he can manipulate his mother but not his father, and he looks at him "uneasily." They seem to have difficulty communicating. His father asks him, "How you n ol man Hawkins gittern erlong?" and Dave answers, "Ah plows more lan than anybody over there." But rather than respond with praise, the father responds with a reprimand: "yuh oughta keep you mind on whut yuh doin." (Students can identify with this conversation: "I got an A- on the Chem exam!" "Well, you'd better pay more attention in class.")

In the second scene with his mother, we learn that Dave's working money is needed to buy clothes for school in the winter. This detail may suggest the family's poverty. That her stocking acts as the family bank might suggest her inability to use a bank (either because of her lack of education or because of legal restrictions) or her mistrust of white-owned institutions. When his mother learns that he wants some money for a gun, she accuses him of having "no sense." But Dave starts to make sense to her when he says that they "need" a gun and plays on her fears about "whut might happen." When she agrees to let him buy the gun on the condition that it be for his father, it becomes apparent that she believes her husband should have a gun. Perhaps his possession of a gun would fulfill his manhood. Or perhaps it would provide protection for the family.

The significance of the gun to Dave is obvious: it gives him "a sense of power" and manhood. He assumes that in authoritative societies, respect is imposed forcefully. And he thinks that the gun will automatically give him respect from everyone, "black or white." Paradoxically, he shows little respect toward his mother, to whom he has promised to give the gun. He deceives her and then sneaks out with the gun. Perhaps rightly so, Mr. Hawkins reacts to Dave's early arrival at the barn "suspiciously."

At the moment when he first shoots the gun, Dave does not act responsibly. He waves it "wildly" and pulls the trigger with his eyes closed. The gun seems to have taken on a life of its own, out of Dave's control. When he realizes he has accidentally hit the mule and that she is dying, he tries in vain to help her. He is compassionate, but at the same time he is reluctant to go for help since he knows the others will figure out what happened.

At the scene of Jenny's burial, Dave tries to deceive people again, even though he knows deep down he cannot fool them. The crowd

31

is "white and black," making Dave feel that everyone is against him. His mother may appear to him to be the worst offender, as it is she who asks about his gun. She is rough on him (perhaps because she believes it is her responsibility to be so until he achieves manhood). His father's action is violent: he "shook him till his teeth rattled." Under this pressure, Dave begins to cry and soon everyone mocks him with laughter. His manhood challenged yet again, Dave is humiliated and humbled, "head down." Even so, he lies again when asked about the location of the gun. At this point, we learn something more about Dave's home life. After his father threatens to beat him, Dave remembers other times when he has been beaten. He sees himself as a mule, an animal who works hard and receives little appreciation. In a sense, in killing the mule, he has killed himself, or at least that self that is subservient and without freedom to act.

Not having learned from his mistake, Dave again attempts to fire the gun. No longer a mule, he is now a "hungry dog," and he is determined to satisfied his need. At first he closes his eyes, but remembering the consequences of that cowardly act, he opens them. Successful this time, from his point of view, he "stood straight and proud." Yet he stills associates manhood with fear, seeing the gun as something to "scare" people with; and he would like nothing better than another bullet to fire at Hawkins's "white" house, symbol of Hawkins's power over him.

At that moment, with little forethought, he hears a train and imagines that to jump the train would mean that he is braver than one of the other men: "Ah betcha Bill wouldn't do it!" Dave may not be thinking clearly; he is "hot all over." But he rejects an oppressive environment and believes that he is heading "somewhere where he could be a man."

Will Dave be able to be a man up north? Some students may say no. He is exposing himself to danger; the gun is "empty"; he has no money; and he is alone. Furthermore, he has an inadequate concept of what it means to be a man. Manhood cannot be achieved through a gun, as the story itself shows. The gun brings tragedy, anger, and despair. Finally, he has acted immaturely by running away from his responsibility. He has left his parents with the burden of repaying his debt. His reactions are childish and impulsive.

On the other hand, some students see Dave's actions in a positive light. Dave might be considered courageous for jumping on a train. He has gained some confidence in shooting the gun properly and overcoming his fear. This courage and confidence may increase his chances to succeed. Should he have stayed home? No. Home is a dead end. His environment does not permit him to reach manhood. Only by leaving does he have any chance to break out of the trap set by the white employer. To mature, he must separate himself from his controlling parents and take charge of his own life. Even if his actions are not ethical (leaving his parents with his debt), within the context of an unjust society, they are defensible. Dave is now free to face the hardships of life alone, as a man. And perhaps the "glinting" rails signal the bright future of his dream.

In the poem "Harlem," Langston Hughes, too, writes about a dream and asks what happens when it is deferred. The answer seems to be either that postponed dreams lose vitality ("dry up"); lead to illness ("fester"); waste away ("decay"); are repressed ("crust and sugar over"); or end in violence ("explode"). Given its title, the poem may refer directly to the dream of racial harmony or justice. Lack of harmony or justice may continue, but its continuation may have a high price. The poem may also refer to any dream, including that of Dave, who dreams of becoming a man. If his dream is deferred, what will be his fate?

(*Note:* An excellent film/video of this story is available through Perspective Films. See page 87 of this manual.)

FURTHER READING

Felgar, Robert. Richard Wright. Boston: Twayne, 1980.
Margolies, Edward. The Art of Richard Wright. Carbondale: Southern
    Illinois U P, 1969.
Stocking, Fred. "On Richard Wright and 'Almos' a Man.'" The
    American Short Story. Vol. 1. Ed. Calvin Skaggs. New York:
    Dell, 1977. 275-81.

"Dead Men's Path" by Chinua Achebe

Summary: A newly appointed headmaster, Michael Obi, is determined to change and modernize what he perceives to be a backward school by maintaining high teaching standards and beautiful grounds. When he closes an ancestral path that crosses the school, a village priest comes to explain the path's importance to the tribe and asks to have it reopened. Obi refuses. The next day he finds much of his school in ruins.

The story takes place in Nigeria in 1949. The school to which Michael is assigned is "unprogressive"; he and his wife are determined to make it "modern." Even their outdoor work attempts to create order out of chaos: they plant beautiful, "carefully tended" gardens among the "rank" bushes of the rest of the neighborhood. The school property acts as a barrier between two sacred places: the village shrine and the villagers' place of burial. This modern school symbolizes an affront to tradition.

Michael is a young man, only twenty-six, but there are hints that he is weighed down and weakened by his responsibility: he is "stoop-shouldered" and "frail" and sits "folded up in a chair." This physical contrast to his apparent inner energy may foreshadow his failure. His condescending attitude toward the villagers is filtered through the narrator's perspective: the school is "backward in every sense of the word"; he is "scandalized" to see an old woman walk through the property; he refers to the teachers in his school as "you people"; and he sees tradition as nothing more than "pagan ritual." Michael is insensitive to the fact that in traditional Igbo culture, to dishonor ancestors is a great offense. He is more concerned about what the authorities will think than he is about what the villagers think. Using "barbed wire" fencing, he simultaneously ostracizes the villagers and, ironically, imprisons himself. Regulations become more important than tradition.

He is not helped in a positive direction by his wife. Nancy's values are materialistic; she is more interested in the outer appearance of the school than she is in its education. That she has been "infected" by modern ideas suggests that they are like a disease. She overestimates her position, seeing herself as "queen," and self-centeredly desires to be envied by others. She talks like a "woman's magazine" rather than a person who can think for herself.

Nancy's use of language is in sharp contrast to the priest's, whose words reflect his native language and culture: "let the hawk perch and let the eagle perch." While Nancy wants to eliminate one way of life, the priest indicates that he wants to make room for both ways. Yet the priest, too, is inflexible. When Michael suggests a compromise--albeit in a cavalier manner--and offers to help build a new path, the priest has "no more words to say." In fact, like Michael, he is described as having a "stoop," suggesting that, like Michael, he is not up to the task of shouldering the responsibility that historical change entails. Neither man has the wisdom or humility needed to fulfill his role.

Having made little or no effort to understand their host community, Michael and Nancy are punished for their misguided notions and superficiality; their hard work is destroyed. Ironically, the "white" supervisor whom Michael had so desired to impress does not view the Obi couple as superior to the villagers. Instead, he lumps them together as a race and nastily refers to their difficulty as a "tribal-war situation." This attitude is typical of colonial administrators, who are ignorant of the ways of Africans. This shared knowledge between author and reader introduces yet another irony into the story: the very people who were determined to modernize Africa were the least equipped to do so.

From the first line of the story--"Michael Obi's hopes were fulfilled much earlier than he had expected"--students might sense that Michael's hope will turn to despair. The narrative voice seems to remain critical of Michael even as it reflects his thoughts. The author's attitude toward Michael and his views might be described as disapproving or mocking. With that analysis, students might conclude that Achebe deplores modernization and criticizes those who ignore tradition. Some students, however, might find the author sympathetic, in that Michael has not been guided well, is young, and must learn from his mistakes. And they might find that the author is not fully sympathetic toward the priest, who ignores his own proverb by refusing to compromise. Likewise, they might question the role of the diviner, who "prescribed heavy sacrifices to propitiate ancestors"--lofty-sounding words--but who does nothing more than allow common vandalism to occur. These analyses might lead to the interpretation that Achebe understands that change is inevitable, but that it needs to accommodate the past, and vice versa.

FURTHER READING

Balogun, F. Ogun. Tradition and Modernity in the African Short Story: An Introduction to a Literature in Search of Critics. New York: Greenwood, 1991. 65-80.

Innes, C. L. Chinua Achebe. Cambridge: Cambridge U P, 1990.

Ogbada, Kalu. Gods, Oracles and Divination: Folkways in Chinua Achebe's Novels. Trenton, NJ: Africa World, 1992.

"Six Feet of the Country" by Nadine Gordimer

Summary: A white South African couple discover that the brother of one of their black farm workers has died on their property. After the post-mortem, the police do not return the body. At the wife's urging, the husband arranges for the body's return for a proper burial; but the pall bearers realize that the body inside the coffin belongs to someone else. The authorities have assumed that any black body will do.

The story is set on a farm ten miles outside of Johannesburg. The owners' social status is marked by their servants and the husband's ownership of a "luxury" travel agency. Yet the farm itself is not luxurious but is characterized by "cattle dip," "mealie-stooks," and "cow-turds." Nevertheless, it represents an escape from the racial tensions of the city, where life is characterized by "guns under the white men's pillows" and "burglar bars on the white men's windows." Still, there is racial division on the farm, where whites call black men "boys" and blacks call their white employer *Baas*.

Lerice, the wife, is described as "plain" and "earthy"; she has no pretenses and is at peace with nature. Her relationship with her husband is weak; apparently, she finds him inadequate because he is jealous of her strength, her "capacity for enthusiasm." Although she has no children of her own, she is maternal, tending to the needs of the workers' offspring. She appears to treat the workers with more equality than her condescending husband is capable of; he finds her attitude "maddeningly logical." She is so caring about the workers that she apparently feels "hurt" when she learns they have not confided in her about the sick man. Her irritation with her husband's cavalier attitude toward the death moves her to silence. She tries to communicate through "alarmed and pressing" eyes, perhaps trying to stop her husband from notifying the authorities; but her husband resists. Yet she defers to her husband, and later expects him to do all the negotiating, because this is not only a white man's world but a white man's world. In the hierarchy of South African society, blacks rate below her, but she rates below her husband.

Petrus seems to fear the man he calls *Baas*. He had not asked for help for his sick brother because of the legal ramifications of his act of giving him sanctuary. He even hesitates before admitting that the dead man was his brother. As he attempts to get his employer to retrieve the body, Petrus behaves "politely," saying "please." He is persistent because he believes in the power of white men, who "have everything, can do anything." His attitude succeeds in making the narrator feel guilty, as they both know that when white men do not do something, "it is because they won't." Petrus is so committed to fulfilling his mission to give his brother a proper burial that he surprises--and irritates--the narrator by raising the twenty pounds needed to pay off the authorities. As a result of the dignity with which he undertakes this mission, Petrus becomes equal to Lerice in the narrator's eyes; both try to communicate with the narrator nonverbally, as though words are useless when dealing with a white man: "for those moments," he says, "they looked

36

exactly alike." For him this "sounds impossible," because he does not recognize their common bond of powerlessness.

All of his life, the narrator has been trying to manage to have it all (symbolized in his city/country existence), but he acknowledges the "impossibility" of that dream. Instead he must settle for a "third" way, in which he never feels fully satisfied with either lifestyle. Although the situation vis-a-vis blacks is less tense on his farm than in the city, his attitude toward the black men is paternalistic. Their relationship is "feudal" and "obsolete" in that the white owners take care of the black workers and the workers have nothing to fear. Although the narrator senses there is something "wrong" with this arrangement, he condescendingly refers to the others as "poor devils." He does not consider that the blacks may not find this arrangement as "comfortable" he does.

His first response to viewing the dead man is emotionless: he sees it as no different from the times when "the boys" stand around the kitchen after a dish is broken. When he learns what has happened, he suspects that this is not the first time the workers have hidden someone. He mocks (or pities) their vision of the "City of Gold," which is no "paradise" but a place of "zoot suits, police raids, and black slum townships." His first instinct is to notify the authorities; this is a person who plays by the rules. Yet even as he does so, he feels defensive about his action in front of his wife: "It might have been something contagious . . . God knows?"

Once he notifies the authorities, we see the political system in action. He himself is under suspicion briefly for having allowed this to happen on his property. Again, a hierarchy is revealed: white police, white man, white woman, black man, in that order. In justifying his relatively fair treatment of blacks, he feels the brunt of the typical nonintellectual response of a racist, someone "possessed by the master-race theory."

The narrator seems to be incapable of dealing with the situation of the body without the urging of his wife. She makes him tell Petrus the truth and she needles him into following up on the case until he succeeds. He is also incapable of understanding the depth of Petrus's anguish. Nor does he value Petrus's traditions, particularly his desire to give his brother a proper burial. The narrator mocks those who make sacrifices to pay for the funeral. Materialistic, he regards life as "something to be spent extravagantly" and death to be "the final bankruptcy." He sees the area with their graves as no more than "bits of broken pottery, a lopsided homemade cross, and jam jars brown with rain water and dead flowers." That each of these objects might originally have been left as a sign of love or respect does not enter his mind.

When he is playing golf--a frivolous act--as the funeral procession begins, however, he feels "awkward." The group and the donkeys leading them are "submissive and downcast." Perhaps the dignity of their movements make him stand "rather foolishly"; he has already recognized the religious air of the procession, which he sees as "Biblical." When he hears the old man's voice, it reminds him of the "mumblings of a prophet," again connecting what he is experiencing with the Bible and religion. When the old man wants to be heard by the symbol of power, the white narrator, he speaks in English. Yet it is this black man who seems "awesome" to the white man, this black man whose mustache is a "symbol of . . . traditional wisdom." After lifting the lid of the coffin, however, the old man "abdicated," giving up his regal stature.

Some students may argue that the narrator has been changed by the experience. Lerice is surprised to find him "so indignant, so determined." He says he is acting on "principle," not something that motivated this rule follower earlier. But other students may point out that Lerice is unimpressed; she just says "Oh" and turns away. And the narrator continues to make jokes about the blacks, comments which he says are "ironic" but which Lerice does not appreciate. Toward the end, he calls the whole episode a "complete waste," perhaps not seeing what he might have gained from it. When he says the old man left "rather better off" because of a secondhand suit, has he missed the point? Or is he being "ironic"?

By using this narrator to tell the story, Gordimer is able to show how essentially good people have difficulty acting on principle; the husband is a weak but not evil man. The system in place is powerful and is difficult to fight. Perhaps the implied message is that much stronger people than the narrator are needed to overcome injustice. Given the narrator's ineffectiveness and the ultimate tragedy for the blacks, the tone of this story will be seen primarily as depressing. Students may see some hope in the author's courage in publishing such a story when she did.

FURTHER READING

Clingman, Stephan. The Novels of Nadine Gordimer: History from the Inside. London: Allen, 1986.
Driver, Dorothy. "Nadine Gordimer: The Politicisation of Women." Critical Essays on Nadine Gordimer. Ed. Roland Smith. Boston: Hall, 1990. 180-204.

Topping, Nancy Bazin, and Marilyn Dallman Seymour, eds. _Conversations with Nadine Gordimer_. Jackson: U P of Mississippi, 1990.

"Like a Bad Dream" by Heinrich Boll

Summary: A man who married into the excavating business is drawn by his wife into a bribery scheme in order to receive a contract for a large housing project. At first, unable to participate, he allows her to make all the arrangements. But ultimately he engages in his own part of the deal, thinking it is "like a bad dream."

From the first sentence, we get a hint of the social setting of the story. The narrator and his wife entertain the Zumpens not so much because they are "nice," but because they are "useful." Social relationships are utilitarian. The drinks and food suggest an upper-class lifestyle: cognac, fancy appetizers, an assortment of cheeses and pastries. The hosts are clearly trying to impress their guests; what is important in this society is knowing "what to offer guests, when to pass the cognac, and when the vermouth." Evidence of the Zumpens' wealth is their uncommon "Italian" car, Mrs. Zumpen's lounging pajamas, and the club at which Mr. Zumpen plays chess. The Zumpen home has expensive religious artworks and the narrator's home contains an antique crucifix. Ownership of these religious artifacts can be seen as ironic, given that these people are involved in unethical behavior.

Another irony in the story is that Bertha was educated by nuns. Yet even the teachings of these religious women focused on superficialities, the kinds of things that women were expected to know at that time in order to be good wives. Some effects of her Catholic schooling remain: she warns her husband "never [to] mention Christ's name in connection with money!" But shortly after, she is willing to use a crucifix to introduce an illegal business deal. And when the deal is actually being made and her husband says "Christ" in the presence of Mrs. Zumpen, Bertha conveniently forgets to reprimand him. Her moral standard is flexible. Most students may see Bertha as demanding, domineering, selfish, unethical, and unlikable to the extent that they feel sorry for the husband. Certainly she manipulates him and gets her way. She even knows when to stay out of his way at appropriate times. But from another perspective, Bertha may be viewed with some sympathy. A daughter, she may have been unable to work in her father's business and therefore can only participate through her husband. She is obviously a sharp, clever woman and may be frustrated.

It may be harder to sympathize with the Zumpens. Already rich, they want more. They seem to be putting their hosts to the test when they ask to see the apartment. They act condescendingly when they see the narrator's "big desk." They have all the right social skills, however. They know when and how to compliment their hosts and how to carry on good dinner conversation, even though it must have been "a frightful bore" to dine with these people. The Zumpens appear to be in cahoots with Bertha. Mrs. Zumpen is expecting them when they arrive, and Mr. Zumpen is conveniently away. Neither of the Zumpens suffer any pangs of guilt or remorse at making this deal.

There is a brief discussion of the narrator's outer and inner characteristics in the section on "Analyzing Key Words and Phrases Related to Character" in Chapter 6. The narrator seems to want the good life as much as any of the other characters do. He likes having a wife who knows how to live with an upper-class crowd. He says they "need the money." Given that they seem to be living well, the implication is that they may be living above their means. Indeed, he feels humbled in the presence of the Zumpens; his own desk "seemed a bit too big" to him. Nonetheless, he is starting to think like a businessman: "it struck me that I could deduct the bottle of cognac from my income tax."

But his wife is dissatisfied with his performance at first. He doesn't know how to engage in these discussions, but he is willing to follow her wherever she goes. Soon their relationship suffers. No longer admiring her, he sees her crudeness in her "primitive" mouth. He is not tempted to kiss her as he usually does. As the deal is being struck, the narrator can barely function: he is in "too much of turmoil to write." After the deal is struck, he looks at the Madonna but cannot understand what he is searching for. Perhaps the Madonna symbolizes the right way, the religious way, the ethical way, but the narrator cannot draw strength from what he sees. He may not have the inner strength to fight back against materialism and corruption. Soon, he makes a better deal with Mr. Zumpen, this time without his wife's help. Then he goes to the kitchen for a glass of milk, not cognac, perhaps reaching for a symbol of the innocence of youth. At the end he says, "I never did understand. It is beyond understanding."

What is beyond understanding? There are many possible interpretations of this line. He may not understand why it is so easy to become corrupt. Why he participated in the bribe. Why he allowed his wife to manipulate him. Why the business world is corrupt. Why money is so powerful. How money changes people. Why he feels guilty. Why he did not stop it when he could have. Why he did not renege. Why his Christian background could not keep him from doing wrong. Why there is such a distance between ideals and reality. Why he never saw this unethical side of his wife before. Why he was so natural in his deal with Zumpen. Whether he is a victim or a perpetrator. And so on.

Note: Some students may not understand the ethical dilemma in this story. In some countries, bribery is an acceptable way of doing business. As some students have told me, it's the only way. When this point comes up in class, a lively debate ensues, usually dealing with legality versus morality.

FURTHER READING

Cunliffe, W. G. "Heinrich Boll's Eccentric Rebels." Modern Fiction
    Studies 21 (1975): 473-79.
Kurz, P. K. "Heinrich Boll: Not Reconciled." On Modern German
    Literature Trans. Mary Frances McCarthy. Tuscaloosa: U of
    Alabama P, 1977. 3-36.
Wilson, A. L. "Art of Fiction: Heinrich Boll." Paris Review 25 (1983):
    67-87.

"Swaddling Clothes" by Mishima Yukio

Summary: A nurse hired to care for a new baby gives birth to her own, illegitimate child in the nursery. The doctor has   the illegitimate child wrapped in loose newspapers, rather than in proper swaddling clothes. Toshiko, in whose home this incident takes places, feels the baby's shame and covers it in flannel. She soon fears that the illegitimate child will grow up to be a criminal and kill her own son. She walks through the park at night, approaches a man lying on a bench covered in newspapers, is grabbed by him, and makes no effort to free herself.

For a discussion of the first paragraph of this story, see pages 74-75 in this manual, under "ACTIVITY: Analyzing key words and phrases related to character."

The husband is Westernized: he has picked out the "Western-style furniture" that Toshiko finds distasteful and he dresses in an "American" style that she finds "garish." Desirous of being the center of attention, he gestures "flamboyantly." Materialistic and unfeeling, he tells how he rescued his "good rug" rather than help

4 1

the nurse, whom he views as nothing more than a "stuck pig." What he finds amusing, Toshiko finds tragic. Toshiko does not tell him about her action because she fears this nonsentimental man would find it "oversoft." Ironically, because of their wealth, Toshiko thinks their life is "too easy, too painless." In fact, he is careless about her feelings and is more interested in spending time with his friends, who are as insensitive as he.

Toshiko, twenty-three years old, seems to feel she deserves her fate, at least partly because of her gender: "what else could a woman expect . . . ?" Her nature is so "oversensitive" that it has affected her physical appearance; thin and delicate, she is more spirit than flesh.

Toshiko is haunted by the image of the baby wrapped in bloodstained newspapers. Depending on one's perspective, this reaction is either compassionate or abnormal. That her husband, his friends, and even the doctor treat the child with scorn suggests the social significance of the illegitimate birth. Such a child in Japan, especially at that time, would have an uncertain future. For the men, this is expected and deserved. For Toshiko, it is disturbing and only increases her guilt about her own privileged life.

Yet Toshiko's concern may extend beyond the bounds of normalcy or at least of a healthy approach to life. She enjoys torturing herself, finding "a certain satisfaction from her somber thoughts." She is perhaps unreasonably concerned about her own son's fate, which in her mind is inexorably bound with the illegitimate baby's. She becomes obsessed with the incident. That she gives herself up to a stranger on a park bench raises many questions. Is this action mentally unbalanced? accidental? foolish? courageous? fated?

The story is set in various places: Toshiko's home, where she is uncomfortable; a nightclub, where she is out of place; the streets of Tokyo; and the park near the palace, which is called an "Abyss." The streets of Tokyo give Toshiko little comfort. The numerous bars suggest frivolity or a degenerate lifestyle. The theater, normally a sign of culture, is characterized by rude patrons and darkness. Even the cherry blossoms in front of the theater give her no pleasure: they are made out of "scraps of white paper," and paper now haunts her. The only light comes from "tall office buildings," symbols of the Westernization of Japan that makes her feel like a stranger.

Toshiko is drawn out of the taxi and into the night by the prospect of viewing the real cherry trees, which represent "purity" and ancient tradition (marked by the colored lanterns), unlike the

paper trees, which for her represent shame and modernity.   Having
lost her fear, this normally "timid and unadventurous" woman darts
between cars until she reaches her goal.   Nevertheless, everything
around her suggests danger: the "pitch black" water, the "somber"
forest, the "solid dark mass" of trees.   Even the blossoms are
drooping "heavily."
      The man on the bench is lying between layers of newspapers.
Psychologically, this factor must cause Toshiko's mind to make the
twenty-year leap from newspaper-swaddled infant to this sleeping
figure.   She sees in this man the infant grown older into someone
who has suffered poverty and difficulty and is now "hopelessly"
immobilized.
      What might the newspapers (both the infant's and the man's)
symbolize?   There are many possible answers.   First, newspapers
are a cheap form of paper, so they may represent low social status.
Newspapers contain the current news of the country and of the
world and therefore represent the modern society that the author
mocks in this story.   Newspapers, once read, are useless; like the
man on the bench, they have no purpose in life.   Newspapers may
symbolize any or all of the following: hopelessness, poverty,
suffering, fate, misery, guilt, shame, unhappiness, humiliation,
injustice, Toshiko's own life.   And so on.

FURTHER READING

Boardman, Gwenn R. "Greek Hero and Japanese Samurai: Mishima's
      New Aesthetic." Critique 12 (1970): 103-15.
Lebra, Joyce C. "Mishima's Last Act." Literature East and West 15
      (1971): 279-98.
Ueda, Makoto. "Mishima Yukio." Modern Japanese Writers and the
      Nature of Literature. Stanford, CA: Stanford U P, 1976. 219-
      59.

      "A Handful of Dates" by Tayeb Salih

      Summary: An adult narrator recalls an incident from his
childhood.   His beloved grandfather, the man who is moved by his
grandchild's recitations from the Koran, acts ruthlessly in his
business relations with their kind neighbor.   At that moment, the
boy feels that he hates his grandfather.
      For a discussion of the first paragraph, see page 75 in this
manual, under "ACTIVITY: Analyzing   key words and phrases
related to setting."

Like "Araby," this story has a dual perspective. The boy has probably not yet reached adolescence as the story begins: people often pat him on the head and pinch his cheek. Yet his visceral reaction at the end suggests that the events of the story mark a turning point from childhood to adolescence. The details he remembers about himself (for example, his innocence) and Masood (for example, his kindness) may suggest that he has turned out to be a sensitive man. That he says "I used to love the mosque" suggests that he has become cynical about religion.

The young boy is sincerely religious. He speaks of the mosque with love and obviously enjoys reciting from the Koran. He also loves nature: he races to the river and fantasizes among the acacia trees. The earth is the "arena for [his] dreams." A favored child, he is devoted to his grandfather and even matches his moods with his idol's, laughing or remaining silent when he senses it is appropriate. His admiration of his grandfather is so profound that he links him with "God's Creation." A curious child, he asks about his neighbor and the meaning of "indolent."

Signs of the boy's mental maturation are evident. For example, when his grandfather's words are at odds with his recollection, the boy begins to question what he hears. Quick and intelligent, his mind is "jostled" by thoughts that suggest that his grandfather is not telling the truth. He knows that Masood has only three wives (acceptable according to Islamic law) but his grandfather's remarks would indicate that he has ninety. He knows, too, that Masood is far from the wealthy man his grandfather describes; and it may occur to him that his grandfather is responsible for Masood's current condition. Frightened by what he is experiencing, he tries to rid his mind of these thoughts. But his mind soon is filled with memories of Masood's concern for nature, a concern so deep that it gave the boy "an inward and unreasoned embarrassment" at having played with the branch of a tree. His emotions deepen as the other boys and men mistreat Masood's property and then divide it up amongst themselves. He thinks of his beloved trees as possessing "a heart that throbbed." Still innocent, "understanding nothing," he does not know why he experiences a sharp pain. The only feeling he can identify is that of hatred toward his grandfather. Unable to express himself verbally, he throws up the dates he has eaten, precisely where he had dreamed of growing up to be like his grandfather. Why does the boy spew up the dates? The Koran teaches that to obtain through tricks or illegal means something that belongs to someone else is to commit a sin. Perhaps the boy is subconsciously trying to rid himself of sin.

While the boy remains confused about his emotions, the adult narrator understands them well. He knows that the boy cannot stand the injustice he witnesses. He provides insight into the boy's reactions through detailed characterizations of Masood and the grandfather.

Despite the fact that his appearance is "shabby," his donkey "lame," his saddle "dilapidated," and his sleeves "torn," Masood is a man with a "beautiful [singing] voice" and a "powerful laugh." He is able to rise spiritually above the poverty of his situation, at least until he is in the presence of the harvesters. Then he isolates himself, standing "aloof." The only time he speaks is to warn someone to be careful not to cut the heart of the palm. For him the trees are "like humans," in that they "experience joy and suffering." Masood is a man who tries to minimize suffering. As he smells the dates, it is clear that he enjoys them for their natural endowments, not for material gain. His bereavement at being deprived of the fruit of his labor is reflected in his eyes, which are jerking about "like two mice that have lost their way home," and in his throat, which is making a noise "like the rasping of a lamb being slaughtered."

The grandfather at first appears to be a kind, religious, and admirable man. Even his physical appearance suggests purity and stature: his beard is "as white as cotton-wool" and he is tall and thin. Everyone looks up to him, literally and figuratively. He regularly prays and enjoys listening to his grandson recite from the Koran. Yet he is not completely truthful about Masood, and he behaves callously toward him. At the mere thought of taking Masood's property, "his eyes sparkled." Ironically, although he calls Masood "indolent," it is he who falls asleep while the others work. Not content to have participated in bringing Masood to this state of degradation, he is unforgiving about the debt, hardly the attitude of the good Muslim described in the Koran.

When students reread the first paragraph, they can focus on the fact that the boy recites *The Chapter of the Merciful;* they may recognize the irony that the man who enjoys hearing these words acts unmercifully toward his neighbor. Some students may defend the grandfather's behavior as an appropriate way to act in business dealings. Others may argue that it does not follow Islamic moral teachings. Most will be sympathetic toward Masood and the boy and find phrases that show that the author is sympathetic as well. Whether the author is sympathetic toward Islam might be subject to debate. The narrator implies that he has lost his love for the

mosque. Has the author? Or is he simply revealing the discrepancy
between religious teachings and actual behavior?

FURTHER READING

Al-Hardallo, Ibrahim. "Sudanese Literature." Encyclopedia of World
    Literature in the 20th Century. Vol. 4. 2nd ed. New York:
    Ungar, 1984. 365-67.
"Salih, Tayeb." African Authors: A Companion to Black African
    Writing. Ed. Donald Herdeck. Washington, DC: Black Orpheus,
    1973. 381.
Smith, Huston. "Islam." The World's Religions. New York:
    HarperCollins, 1991. 221-70.

"The Plane Reservation" by Massud Farzan

Summary: A young man returns home to Iran after having
studied in the United States for several years. The differences
between himself and his parents are glaring. Once he has satisfied
himself that his parents are "a bit happier" than he remembered
them to be, he makes a plane reservation to leave.

For a discussion of the first paragraph of this story, see page 78
in this manual under the heading "ACTIVITY: Analyzing key words
and phrases related to point of view."

The street on which Morad's family lives is "narrow," literally
and figuratively. As Morad returns to his home, his mood reflects
the name of his street, Sadness. He must pass through a "dark
vestibule" and when he sees his mother, after ten years of
separation, he feels no joy. Through his perspective as a young man
who has lived abroad, he sees the house as having "no furniture"
other than a chair which has been placed there only to
accommodate him. The house itself reflects his native culture: thick
rugs and a prayer-spread. It also reflects the relative primitiveness
of his family's life in Iran: the outdoor toilet has neither stool nor
seat.

Morad's mother is a religious woman. When she first sees her
son, she thanks Allah and finishes her prayers. Morad notices that
the chador is longer and her rosary bigger than he had
remembered, suggesting that she has become even more religious
as she has aged. He also remembers some negative things about
her; for example, she was prone to making "snide remarks" to his
father and seemed to take pleasure in disturbing this man whom
she refers to as a "bad vessel." Her comment that she expected her

son to come back from America "fat and white" may make her seem ignorant, backward, and/or materialistic. But some students who have had this experience may be amused by this scene. Like many parents, the mother is disillusioned when her expectations are not fulfilled. She agrees with her husband on the need for Morad to look more like a gentleman, but otherwise she is reluctant to share experiences with her husband (she watches him "from the corner of her eye") or to let him know her true feelings ("she didn't want father to see the broad smile").

Morad's father seems a bit more complex. A failed inventor, he is the object of his wife's contempt and frustration. Nevertheless, Morad remembers that his father spent much of his time reflecting and inventing, dreaming of making money. Morad believes that if they became rich, his father would invest in nature, fulfill his religious obligations, become charitable, incur respect, and secure his future in the world beyond. Whether these nonmaterialistic values and goals are those of Morad or of his father is subject to debate. Perhaps this is wishful thinking on Morad's part, for his father's values do seem to be superficial when Morad returns. Like his wife, he focuses on Morad's outer characteristics and judges him. For him, respect is tied to wealth or at least the appearance of wealth. Students can discuss to what extent this is a cultural difference (the father does say that he is only telling Morad what is important "in this country") and to what extent it is a personal value. This same man, however, has spiritual qualities: he quotes poetry and accepts as Allah's will those things that cannot be changed. On the other hand, he has abandoned his creative side, his inventiveness, and now tries to get something with no effort through the lottery. His apparent joy at having won a mere dollar and twenty-five cents may indicate the compromises he has had to make in life.

Morad is not only caught between cultures but also must deal with mixed emotions (perhaps symbolized by the intersecting streets: Sadness and Pomegranate Blossoms). Apparently, he has returned with the possibility of staying: he has no plane reservation back to the States and he tells his mother he may marry in Iran. But, from the beginning, he feels out of place, a stranger in his own land. He claims that he is "not a foreigner" but then he acts like one: he pays the cabdriver more than necessary. He has grown so tall that he no longer fits in his own home. He tries to readjust to the cultural life of the family by sitting on the rugs, and for a while it even "feels so good" to spread his legs. Then he cannot help but remember the discomfort that pervaded his childhood home, the parents who could not understand one another or treat each other with kindness. He is not at ease with either of them, nor they with him. He has little chance to discuss anything important with them, as they can speak of nothing but his disappointing appearance. Yet, in his maturity, he "didn't resent that at all." He seems to understand them better than they understand themselves or him. He is motivated by a desire to help his parents and to see if they "forgave each other's foibles." Whether they actually are happier is subject to debate. (Does his mother's "broad smile" reveal pleasure or mockery?) The fact that Morad snaps a picture of them stringing beans "together in peace and harmony" suggests that he wants to freeze that moment. Perhaps the photo reflects the real thing. Or perhaps taking that picture is just the way that Morad deceives himself and gives himself permission to leave.

By planning to have his shoes shined, Morad is doing something that will please them and/or that will symbolically show his accommodation to his country's values. Depending on one's perspective, the shining of shoes may represent bringing the best of his culture back to the States.

Interestingly, we learn very little about Morad the child. What was he like? Why did he leave? What did he do in the United States? Why didn't he return sooner? etc. Students can speculate on why the author omits this information. They can also discuss whether a son can reliably analyze his parents' situation, especially when he has such ambivalence and conflicting emotions.

In some respects, this is an achingly honest portrayal of a marriage. Students may feel either contempt or sympathy toward the father, mother, and/or Morad, depending on their own experiences.

FURTHER READING

"Farzan, Massud." Contemporary Authors. Vols. 53-56. Ed. Claire
    Kinsman. Detroit: Gale, 1975. 187-88.
Hamalian, Leo, and John D. Yohannan, eds. "The Persian
    Background." New Writing from the Middle East. New York:
    Ungar, 1978. 273-78.
"Iranian Literature." Encyclopedia of World Literature in the 20th
    Century. Vol. 2. 2nd ed. New York: Ungar, 1982. 453-56.

"The Verb *to Kill*" by Luisa Valenzuela

Summary: A young narrator talks about a man she fears will rape and kill her. At the end of the story, after she states she has been given a hunting rifle, she says the man "has been killed."

The clever way in which the story is written lends itself to various interpretations. Beginning with the conjugation of the verb *to kill,* it introduces fear, humor, or suspense, depending on one's perspective.

Who is this man who so obsesses the narrator? He is someone that she and her sister see on the beach, someone they fear because he looks "like a murderer" with his "long bushy hair and gleaming eyes." He spends his time gathering pebbles, which they assume are to "cover up the graves of his victims." He looks at them when they walk on the beach and they are so frightened that they are paralyzed in place until he passes. When he "suddenly showed up" one day, they panic. They notice his bizarre behavior in talking to lettuce and surmise that he's "crazy." They are convinced he is planning to kill them.

Yet a closer look at the details provided about the man shows that he does absolutely nothing to them. In fact, he usually walks right by them and does not even notice what they are doing. His interest in pebbles seems to be aesthetic: he holds the transparent ones up to the sun. He attracts animals, a quality that is almost universally considered to be a positive one. Ironically, it is the girls who are less than kind: they eat the injured seagull. That he talks affectionately to plants indicates that he cares about nature's gifts. All in all, from a perspective other than the narrator's, he appears to be gentle man.

What does this say about the narrator, then? Young and innocent, using terms like "peepee," she is cared for ("well nourished") and protected by her mother. The way she fills her time seems to be age-appropriate: she digs for clams on the beach and talks for hours with her sister. Yet there is a dark side to her. She spends an inordinate amount of time thinking about murder and sexual molestation. And she has mean thoughts about another young girl, whom she hopes will be caught by the murderer but not sexually abused because "she might like it." Given that she is playful yet sexually aware, she may be at the crossroads of adolescence. Unfortunately, her sexual awakening--the "shiver" that is "lower down" in her body and "stimulating"--is linked to deviant behavior. Why? Apparently she is influenced by newspaper reports of "degenerates." Here, females are seen as powerless victims, nothing more than the prey of animalistic men. It is interesting for students to compare her sexual awakening with that of the boy in "Araby," who links love to a religious quest (one student wrote a fascinating comparative paper on this subject, examining the different social influences on the development of male and female sexuality).

Ironically, though the narrator says that she would be "ashamed to tell anybody" about the "repulsive" things the rapist would do to her, there seems to be nothing too shameful for her to tell us. Her descriptions of the violence are vivid, as she thinks about the man "plunging a knife in [Pocha's] belly" or putting "in our mouths that terrible thing we know he has."

What happens at the end of this story is subject to debate. Some students are convinced that she kills the man with the rifle her father gives her, which ironically was given as a reward for doing well in school; they think that she has learned her lessons well. They find evidence of her callous tendency when she eats the injured seagull. These students find the story horrifying. Other students, agreeing that she kills the man, see her as a heroine, someone who saves other girls from being attacked. Others see the story as a tragedy about how fear can turn to aggression. Yet others find the story to be wildly funny, entirely a figment of an impressionable girl's imagination. The seagull incident is seen as humorous: "A little tough, but tasty." Yet others agree that it is a figment of her imagination, but do not find it funny. They believe that what she kills is her imagination, that as she becomes sexually aware, she must leave her childhood behind. Or they think that she has killed her fear. That is the lesson she learns.

Students may see a great deal of symbolism in the story, some of which crosses cultures. For example, in one exchange, a student from Spain said that in Mediterranean cultures, the clam is related to a women's sexual organs; a student from Thailand said that it was true in her country too; an American student added that it is used as slang in English; and three other students mentioned the clam in paintings/sculptures of Venus. This discussion prompted a student to mention the rabbits as another sexual symbol of fertility. Another student asked whether that meant that the girl wanted to put an end to sex by hunting rabbits. Another suggested she wanted to kill the man to stop sex. At that point, a Latino male student said that in Latin countries girls do not know much about sex; they would prefer to die rather than to have it!

One student who viewed the story as a "funny and classy" tale about self-centered adolescent girls began his essay with a line reminiscent of Valenzuela's style: "Everyone has, everyone had, everyone will have, everyone has had, ignorant imaginings or dreams when one is, one was, one will be, one has been, a teenager."

FURTHER READING

Magnarelli, Sharon. Reflections/Refractions: Reading Luisa
    Valenzuela New York: Lang, 1988.
Marting, Diane. "Female Sexuality in Selected Short Stories by Luisa
    Valenzuela: Toward an Ontology of Her Work." Review of
    Contemporary Fiction 6 (1986). 48-54.
"Valenzuela, Luisa." World Authors: 1980-1985. Ed. Vineta Colby.
    New York: Wilson, 1991. 860-63.

"Girl" by Jamaica Kincaid

Summary: "Girl" is a series of instructions to a girl.
Although there is no direct mention of country, "Girl" is set in Antigua. Hints of the West Indies milieu are provided in the references to music, clothing (khaki shirt and pants), foods, plants, and superstitions ("don't throw stones at blackbirds," which action, I was told, is believed to result in illness). Depending on one's perspective, the fact that the girl is told to dry clothes on the "stone heap" may suggest poverty; on the other hand, few tropical countries have need for machine dryers.

Over what period of time the story takes place is subject to debate. Students may view the directives as the words of a mother to her daughter spoken quickly, perhaps in anger (many students have heard such a string of words after they have done something wrong). Other students believe the mother speaks over a long period of time, that the instructions cover the girl's childhood, adolescence, and impending adulthood. Yet others feel that the piece reflects the perspective of the girl, in that the structure (one long sentence) suggests a young woman's transcription or interpretation of the seemingly unending string of commands remembered over a lifetime.

The story contains numerous images that enable readers to form mental pictures: "try to walk like a lady"; "don't squat down to play marbles"; "always squeeze bread to make sure it's fresh," etc. So many details are provided that the characters' own world and values come alive; yet at the same time universal recognition is possible. Women across cultures receive recipes similar to these, about the proper way to be a woman in society. Students may at first be taken aback by the use of the word *slut* (some may claim that a mother would never use such a term and that therefore the speaker must be some other adult), but then realize that much of the information that girls receive from their mothers is provided to prevent them from becoming sexually active before marriage. Males, too, receive messages about what it means to be a man or to be manly. Students can benefit from writing down the instructions they themselves have received concerning their gender roles or other roles or identities (such as family or other relationships, ethnicity, religion, job, culture, sports), discussing them and comparing them, in content and style, to Kincaid's piece. In doing so, they may understand better the way in which style can reflect meaning. Some students see the style as reflecting a negative impression. The one-sentence format throws information at readers constantly, barely giving us a chance to take a breath. By condensing all the details into one paragraph, the author provides an oppressive atmosphere. Other students see the style as reflecting a sense of humor. By stringing together so many of the commands they recognize from their own experiences, they find the author's words true to life and funny.

Depending on how they view the overall tone of the piece, students will have different assessments of the characters. While there may not be agreement on whether one of the characters is the girl's mother, there is little doubt that one of the characters is a girl (or at least a girl who has grown into a woman). That girl may be seen as passive, primarily listening to all of the instructions and speaking only to prove that she is a good girl: *"but I don't sing benna on Sundays at all."* Or she may be seen as fearful that no matter what she does, she will fail to fulfill expectations: *"but what if the baker won't let me feel the bread?"* Yet these same lines may suggest that she is somewhat rebellious, challenging the adult who is speaking to her. She may feel that she has no freedom to change the rules of behavior. She is given little opportunity even to speak. Depending on one's perspective, she can be seen as an oppressed individual, a victim of a social system that has predetermined women's roles. Or she can be seen as a greatly loved and valued child, one whose mother gives her survival skills to protect her from harm. Or both.

The mother (or mother-figure) is also fulfilling a woman's role: passing on her wisdom to her daughter. Whether this is viewed as a positive or a negative phenomenon depends on one's ideology. Again, those students who find the story humorous or touching may be reassured by the passing on of tradition from generation to generation. Those who find it disturbing may see the mother as overbearingly authoritative and demanding, passing on not a positive tradition but perpetuating the institutionalized oppression of women. Or they may see her as dysfunctional, a victim herself of the constraints of society and now passing on a cycle of abuse. Perhaps she is frustrated by the role she has had to play as a woman and takes that frustration out on the child. Perhaps she feels competitive toward this developing young woman and angry that she is losing control of her.

FURTHER READING

"Kincaid, Jamaica." Current Biography Yearbook. Ed. Charles Moritz.
    New York: Wilson, 1991. 330-33.
Kincaid, Jamaica. A Small Place. New York: Farrar, 1988.
Niesen de Abruna, Laura. "Twentieth-Century Women Writers from
    the English-Speaking Caribbean." Modern Fiction Studies 34
    (1988): 85-96.

"A Woman Like Me" by Xi Xi

Summary: A woman is waiting in a coffee shop for her boyfriend, Xia, to show him for the first time where she works. He knows that she is a cosmetician but does not know that her clients are cadavers. She believes that Fate has predetermined that Xia will reject her. At the end of the story, he approaches.

For an analysis of the opening lines, see pages 79-80 of this manual, under "ACTIVITY: Analyzing diction and sentence development."

Neither the coffee shop nor the funeral home is described in any detail. Clues about Chinese culture are embedded in the details provided by the narrator, however: the names of the characters (for example, Xia, whose name means "eternal summer"), the influence of Fate, the taboo of death, the expected role of woman (passive, sweet). The story takes place on a Sunday morning, during which the narrator recollects her life.

Clearly this is a time when women can have a life outside the home. Xia is undeterred when he learns the narrator is a working woman. After all, this is a "modern, civilized society." Yet only certain jobs are acceptable: "a teacher, a nurse, or a secretary or clerk." Options for a woman without qualifications for these jobs are limited; she can "work as a saleswoman in a shop . . . sell bakery products, or . . . be a maid in someone's home." Women are expected to work at jobs that are "intimate, graceful, and elegant." That the narrator has a job working with the dead is unacceptable. She loses all her friends when they learn what she does. For them, she represents "the ghost of their own inner fears."

Fearless, Aunt Yifen has raised the narrator from childhood and passed on her skills to her because she, too, has no fear. Pale and slow-moving, Aunt Yifen has become "uncommunicative" because her lover lacked courage and therefore love. Perhaps because of her own disappointment, she believes strongly that her niece should be independent of men and "never have to rely upon anyone else to get through life." Depending on one's perspective, the aunt can be seen as a strong role model, one who shows the way to a specially selected apprentice. But she can also be seen as a limiting force in the narrator's life, one whose superstitious "premonition" that their fates are inexorably linked gives the narrator little choice and little hope.

Outwardly, the narrator thinks she has the appearance of a "happy person," but her position in the "shadowy corner" of the coffee shop reflects her inner despair. She is an extraordinarily complex character, one given to contradictions. She says "there is no escape" from the "trap" set by Fate; yet she criticizes those who "stupidly" resign themselves to "Fate's whims." She claims that Fate controls her life; yet she says she is to "blame" for her situation, seeing it as her "fault." She says she has a "natural inability to express what I think and feel"; yet early in her relationship with Xia, she "expressed her feelings toward him without holding back a thing." (As listeners to her tale, students can evaluate her ability to express herself.) She says she "lack[s] self-control"; yet she has been careful to control the amount of information she gives to Xia (and she controls the tone of her tale). She claims to be a woman "with little knowledge"; yet she intelligently discusses a broad range of philosophical topics, including fate, fear, death, courage, love, suicide, and the meaningless of human existence. (Close examination of her views on any of these topics may reveal more contradictions.)

Given these contradictions, students must analyze deeply in order to understand this character. Some may be disgusted with her for being passive and submitting to fate. Others, noting her Chinese heritage, may look at her through that cultural lens and be sympathetic toward her plight. Her job is an extreme violation of culturally acceptable images of women: she deals daily with death, a taboo subject; and she touches naked male bodies. Some may argue that she despises womanhood and femininity. Others may argue that she is far from passive, that she is in fact a courageous person who resists social norms. She is determined to "take firm strides in life."

Most of the people in the story lack courage: Aunt Yifen's boyfriend, the narrator's former friends, the deceased who meekly accepted their lot. In fact, the society in which the narrator lives is far from admirable: it is full of "worldly bickerings . . . petty jealousies, hatreds . . . [and] disputes over personal fame or gain." Her job exists because people need to be "deceived by appearances," to cover up what they really look like, who they are. Ironically, death has a leveling effect, bringing everyone, "rich or poor, high or low," to the same state. Ironically, too, in the eyes of others she is "cold," when in fact it is they, the representatives of a "greed-consumed, dog-eat-dog world," who deserve that label.

What, then, of Xia? According to the narrator, he is "happy," a man "who exists in a world of brightness." She assumes, therefore, that he will not want to spend his life with a woman who is "surrounded by darkness." She also claims to believe that she is destined to share Aunt Yifen's fate, yet she suggests that "maybe somewhere there is a man of true courage." Perhaps it is Xia. Even though she says the outcome is a "foregone conclusion," she has gone to great lengths to hint at the possibility of resisting fate. Had she truly believed he would flee, would she have bothered to test him? She notes that Xia brings the sun with him; perhaps she hopes he will eliminate the shadow. Ironically, the flowers that represent happiness to Xia mean grief for her. Yet, given that she speaks in contradictions, why should we believe that this is true? Perhaps the entire tale is created to provide the very "self-protection" that she claims she has "no concept" of.

FURTHER READING

Chang, Sung-sheng Yvonne. "Three Generations of Taiwan's Women Writers." Bamboo Shoots after the Rain: Contemporary Stories by Women Writers of Taiwan. Ed. Ann C. Carver and Sun-Sheng Yvonne Chang. New York: Feminist, 1990. xv-xxv.

Chung, Ling. "Perspectives and Spatiality in the Fiction of Three Hong Kong Women Writers." Modern Chinese Women Writers: Critical Appraisals. Ed. Michael S. Duke. Armonk, NY: Sharpe, 1989. 217-35.

Duke, Michael, ed. Introduction. Worlds of Modern Chinese Fiction. Armonk, NY: Sharpe, 1991. vii-xiii.

"The Street-Sweeping Show" by Feng Jicai

Summary: Led by the mayor and other public figures, citizens clean the huge city square as part of National Cleanup Week. After the television cameras are turned off, the mayor leaves in his limousine.

Because everyone is out sweeping the streets, the air is "thick with dust"; like the atmosphere, the truth is being covered up. The dignitaries pick a section of concrete pavement that was "clean to begin with"; though they are praised for working, their actions are meaningless. A foolish sight to the narrator (and comical to most readers), they artificially chase the only piece of litter available. The old-fashioned wheelbarrows carrying bamboo brooms are in sharp contrast to the limousines that carry the VIPs. Protected from everyday life, the hypocritical leaders of the community need associate with "grime" only briefly. Soon they are whisked off in cars that smell pleasantly of "gasoline and leather" to homes with servants and scented soap. (Membership in the Communist party conferred significant benefits to those with political status.)

Far from being egalitarian, this society fosters not only class differences but also gender differences. This is a man's world. Only two female dignitaries are invited, and only after the oversight is discovered. The mayor may say that "women are the pillars of society," but they are noticeably absent from committees and federations dealing with literature and art, trade, youth, and athletics. Women are an important part of the work force but have little authority except in a women's organization.

Secretary Zhao is the perfect apparatchik. He wears his requisite Mao suit (official policy in China emphasized that an interest in clothing and style indicated dangerous bourgeois tendencies). Outwardly, he appears "gentle, deferential"; his voice is "modulated" and his attire "utilitarian." But inside he is "shrewd, hard-driving." He understands his position in the hierarchy and does the mayor's bidding.

The mayor is a more complex character. He, too, attends to the details of his position: he pores over lists and even approves menus; this is a sign of "true leadership." Like Secretary Zhao, he knows his place in the hierarchy. He treats the secretary like a student and adopts a regal stature, allowing Zhao to open the door for him and to replace his broom. In front of others, he understands that, as mayor, he must "set an example"; but he does so only to be popular: he fulfills his political role by smiling and shaking hands. In this

56

role he knows better than to speak in anything but clichés: "Everyone should pitch in to clean up our city." At the end of the story we realize that he knows it has just been a sham when his language becomes honest: "It's not worth watching." He sets an example for his grandson, not as "an actor, putting on a show," but as a role model for family values.

Ironically, although the mayor does not value his work, he may in fact be a good influence on ordinary people (that is, those who are not in power). Not only the onlookers but also the television audience will have the opportunity to see him set an example of community action. Usually, when there is a campaign such as this one, it is necessary to get the public's attention, to encourage them to participate and feel good about what they do. For that reason, the mayor knows he must play his part. And so the system continues.

FURTHER READING

Chen, Susan Wilf. Introduction. Chrysanthemums and Other Stories. by Feng Jicai. San Diego: Harcourt, 1985. 1-13.
"Feng Jicai." World Authors: 1980-1985. Ed. Vineta Colby. New York: Wilson, 1991. 279-81.
Link, Perry. Introduction. Stubborn Weeds: Popular and Controversial Chinese Literature after the Cultural Revolution. Bloomington: Indiana U P, 1983. 1-28.

"The Grass-Eaters" by Krishnan Varma

Summary: The narrator describes his life in Calcutta, where he has lived with his wife on a footpath, in a freight wagon, in a concrete pipe, and on a roof. In their old age, they have few clothes and subsist primarily by eating grass. The narrator expresses contentment.

At the point that the narrator tells us the story, he is an old man. Yet the story spans many years, beginning with the early years of his marriage. (Note: There's a tricky time switch between the thirteenth and fourteenth paragraphs. One minute Prodeep is a child and the next he is grown; the present tense is used for both scenes.)

Many details provide a vivid picture of Calcutta. It is so crowded that people live in a footpath. Lacking good health care and adequate living conditions, children die young. The economic situation is so bad that even a school teacher has no roof over his

57

head (this detail could also be connected to the status of teachers in India). The elderly have few clothes and almost nothing to eat. The trams are crowded. In certain areas, violence and looting are a way of life. The political situation is anarchic and inflammatory: at protest meetings, they "denounce British imperialism, American neo-colonialism, the central government, capitalism and socialism, and set off crackers"; in fact, the imposition of these Western-based ideas is at the root of many problems. Not everyone shares this fate, of course. Some characters are well fed: "spherical" and "ovoid."

Swapna is a woman who is well prepared to defend against impropriety; "fangs bared, claws out," she punishes her husband for touching another woman. More conservative than her husband, she likes when things stay fixed in place; she wants to raise a family in a "stationary home," for stability. More traditional, she rejects Western-style practices such as kissing.

Ajit Babu has a liberated mind; he's unconventional, especially by Western standards. No matter what the circumstances of his life, he enjoys sex (the freight wagon gives them "complete freedom to make love day or night"); maintains a sense of humor ("Did I think she was a frog?"); sustains a sense of self-worth ("our life together has been very eventful"); and always looks on the bright side ("we don't get nibbled by rats and mice and rodents as often as they do"). His values are simple: to survive and to have a son to perform funeral rites. At the point where the story leaves off, he is surviving and his son still lives.

Does this mean that he has achieved his goals? This question may reflect too Western a concept. One student noted that in American literature, characters typically have a dream (often the proverbial American Dream) and work hard to attain it. In this story, the character is simply satisfied with what he has; he does not seem to be striving for anything. Students can discuss the cultural differences that emerge here and the forces (e.g., Hinduism) that may engender them. Students who believe that striving is an essential component of human nature will interpret this story differently from students brought up in cultures that assume people should accept their lot in life.

Students may divide sharply on the tone of the story. Many find it sad, melancholic, tragic. They are devastated to learn about the extreme crowdedness and poverty of the city and reflect on their own relatively comfortable life. Others find the story wildly funny, for example, because the author, through exaggeration, describes exactly the stereotypes people have about India. Or because he uses black humor to depict the characters' situation: for example, Ajit Babu doesn't mind having only one leg because he can save on footwear.

FURTHER READING

Lapierre, Dominique. The City of Joy. New York: Doubleday, 1985.
Smith, Huston. "Hinduism." The World's Religions. New York:
    HarperCollins, 1991. 12-81.
Walsh, William. Introduction. Indian Literature in English. London:
    Longman, 1990. 1-30.

"Las papas" by Julio Ortega

Summary: A man living in the United States cooks dinner, and as he slices potatoes (las papas), he is reminded of his native Peru. As his young son moves in and out of the kitchen to check on the progress of the meal, he recalls how he once had rejected his own father's cooking. Noting that the "entire history of his people" is contained in the potato, he plants one in the ground as his son watches.
The story takes place in September. As he looks out the window, the man's complex emotions are reflected in the wind that hints at fall (he feels "the agony of emotions not easily understood") and in the "calm, repeated blue" sky (he discovers "a symmetry in the repetitions" of parental behavior). As he reflects on his present, we learn that he is a single parent who has learned how to provide a family atmosphere for his son. As he reflects on his past, we learn about the importance of his own family life.

The potatoes cause him to indulge in a remembrance of things past. At first he is conscious only of their physicality: their coloring and weight. Then he wonders about their origin. Soon he compares them to those of his native country, Peru. Noting that many varieties of potatoes have been lost, he connects the loss with political upheavals and the pillaging of the land. Potatoes symbolize the country's underdevelopment, and so as a youngster he rejected them, as he later was to retreat from Peru in favor of the developed world.

Suddenly, the potato in his hand is transformed into another symbol of his past, one connected to his childhood, one that "belonged to him." The potatoes represent an "unfinished history," a link with his father (papa), an awareness of the inevitable cycle of parental love and parent/child conflict. In rejecting his father's cooking, he rejected his father's values. He now sees his responsibility not only to give his son unconditional love, as his own father had done, but also to provide access to the culture and background he himself had received: he switches from an Italian to a Peruvian recipe. By planting the potato, he sinks his roots in and propagates his own culture on American soil. Ironically (intentionally or not), given that the potato grows underground, it may act as a symbol of the "marginal spaces" that immigrant cultures occupy in America.

The potato, too, represents the man's identity. As a combination of ingredients (Peruvian and American), he represents an "illusion" of the melting pot. In truth, he now realizes, each flavor can still be deciphered. Like the potato, he can stay "true to [his] own internal form," his Peruvian culture, even as he has "adapted" to a different land, a new environment.

FURTHER READING

Dobyns, Henry E., and Paul L. Doughty. Peru: A Cultural History. New York: Oxford U P, 1976.
Ortega, Julio. Poetics of Change: The New Spanish-American Narrative. Austin: U of Texas P, 1984.
Shapard, Robert, and James Thomas, eds. Afternotes. Sudden Fiction International. New York: Norton, 1989. 331.

"Village" by Estela Portillo Trambley

Summary: A Mexican-American soldier in Vietnam, reminded by a village of his own barrio back home, refuses to follow orders to destroy the village. To prevent the action, Rico shoots his sergeant in the arm. He is arrested but feels free.

The story begins at dawn. The village that he observes from a bluff is "peaceful" and reflects the "intimacy" that a close neighborhood engenders. He recognizes the universality of human existence as he watches a woman carrying a child. Even the physical environment is similar to one he knows well: the "same scent . . . same warmth from the sun." The stillness in Vietnam is the "same kind of stillness" he knew in the barrio.

These images are in sharp contrast to the images of war that also surround him. The stillness is broken by the thunderous sounds of military helicopters. The people of Vietnam have been dehumanized by Americans through military training and language: they are nothing more than rib cages needing to be stomped upon or throats needing to be strangled. Their homes are not really homes but "hootches"; their villages are merely "good pyre for napalm." In an inversion of normal moral teachings, these ideas are contained in a "combat bible."

Such dehumanization is easy for characters like Sergeant Keever. He does not question orders or analyze what he is doing. Rico's questions are just an irritation for him, something that must be dealt with, but perfunctorily. He speaks the language of a stereotypical B-movie soldier: "move your ass . . . . Get back to your position soldier or I'll shoot you myself . . . . That fucking bastard-- get him." Capable of ignoring the humanity of the Vietnamese, he is also capable of ignoring Rico's humanity: "Sergeant Keever had already erased him from existence." A rebellious soldier, according to his moral standard, deserves no more consideration than the enemy.

Rico is quite transparent. From the beginning he has resisted the manipulation of the army, into which he was most likely drafted: "He had been transformed into a soldier, but he knew he was no soldier." The spiritual values he learned from his mother in the barrio, the appreciation for all forms of nature, cannot be erased; he knows what matters: human life, "like the earth and sun."

Depending on one's perspective, Rico is either a traitor or a hero. Some students are disgusted with him, finding him to be pretentious and self-righteous, a loser no matter how he perceives himself. They see his attitude as inappropriate during a time of war, as it puts his fellow soldiers at great risk. Even his anti-killing morality is considered suspect: "It was not killing the enemy that his whole being was rejecting, but firing machine guns into a village of sleeping people." If he is such a humanitarian, they argue, why does he not reject the idea of killing anyone? Students may also discuss the morality of war itself; what is good or bad behavior during normal times can be the opposite during a time of war. War, they may argue, has its own rules and laws. Not to follow them is to break a bond.

Other students feel that Rico's own perceptions of what he does are what is important. That he feels "free" while in prison indicates that his conscience is clear. They argue that someone must defy orders if orders are against a universal moral code (a concept that requires much discussion). They respect what he has done (although some of them say they would not want a soldier like him in their platoon).

Is Rico patriotic? Of course, the answer to this question depends on students' definitions of patriotism. If it means love of country and its values, then yes, Rico loves his country, a place where he has the freedom and opportunity to fulfill his beloved mother's dream. If it means following his leaders, then no, Rico is not a patriot.

Some students may be furious with the author, whom one described as a "very good example of what people think when they haven't served in the army and watch a lot of movies." Such students say she has no clue about a soldier's responsibility; she is naive. Students can discuss the author's awareness of the complexity of Rico's decision. She does leave several clues to suggest that Rico is putting his fellow soldiers at risk. For example, it was quite common to find deadly traps in apparently peaceful towns. Can she admire him for what might have been an action with tragic consequences for his fellow soldiers, mostly innocent inductees like himself?

Perhaps this is less a story about Rico and more a story about the way in which war creates more victims than heroes.

FURTHER READING

Bruce-Novoa. "Estela Portillo." Chicano Authors: Inquiry by Interview. Austin: U of Texas P, 1980. 163-81.
"Portillo Trambley, Estela." Chicano Literature: A Reference Guide. Ed. Julio A. Martinez and Francisco A. Lomeli. Westport, CT: Greenwood, 1985. 316-22.
Lattin, Vernon E., and Patricia Hopkins. "Crafting Other Visions: Estela Portillo Trambley's New Rain of Scorpions." Estela Portillo Trambley. Rain of Scorpions and Other Stories. Binghamton, NY: Bilingual Press/Editorial Bilingue, 1993. 1-14.

PART THREE: WRITING AN ESSAY

Part Three takes up a significant part of The International Story because I am committed to the idea of providing a lot of writing instruction. Nevertheless, a cautionary note: Neither instructor nor student should follow to the letter either the content or the order of the material in this book. In defining expectations, I have tried to focus on the underlying assumptions of writing an interpretive essay, not on a rigid formula or format. In fact, my experience has been that once students have a basic framework, they can create texts that may not follow explicit guidelines but that are still effective.

CHAPTER 5: Writing an Interpretive Essay

Students in the composition and literature course I teach over a fifteen-week semester usually write four essays in addition to keeping a reading log and literary journal (and doing an independent poetry, novel, or research project).

I have included three different essay assignments in this section. The assignments do not necessarily need to be given in this order. In some classes, it might be best for students to write each essay about only one story. In other classes, writing about two or more stories after the first assignment or throughout the semester may be preferable, especially if the stories are presented according to a thematic scheme (see THEMATIC ARRANGEMENT OF STORIES on page 85 in this manual). With such an approach, students may draw from several stories to write about a personally significant event or idea. Or they may select a theme common to several stories and show how different authors have dealt with the topic. (See also pages 64-65 in this manual for alternative approaches.)

DEFINING THE AUDIENCE

Although there was a time when I thought that I was open to student experimentation with no boundaries, I now own up to the reality that - I have certain expectations when I ask students to fulfill assignments. And so I have found it useful to give students the opportunity to "interview" me about the assignments.

The first question asks, "What does the instructor already know about the subject matter?" One thing they know is that I "know" the stories in the sense that I have read and analyzed them on numerous occasions. What I emphasize is that I am interested in learning how _they_ view the stories. Each student can bring a unique perspective to bear on the readings and enable me to see the stories in ways I had not previously imagined. To answer the questions about why they should repeat details and quotations that are well known to me, I explain that it is an issue of orienting the reader: I need for them to make clear where they are in the text of the story. I remind them that they might interpret a detail/quotation differently from the way I do, and that I need to see the detail/quotation in their essay, next to their interpretation, in order to understand what they see and why. I ask for page numbers so that I can refer back to the original easily.

EXPLORING A TOPIC

There are many suggestions in this section for finding and developing a topic and I doubt that any student or instructor could find the time to work with all of them, especially not for one essay assignment. As with everything else in The International Story, the guidelines are provided to suggest possibilities, not to present rigid rules to follow.

I leave class time for students to explore their topics; sometimes whole periods are "Writing Workshops." They can reread stories; take notes; brainstorm; ask questions; talk in pairs or groups about their writing; start or revise a trial draft; and so on. My experience has been that those students who need to will refer to the book; others can function well just on the basis of what is done in class.

WRITING A TRIAL DRAFT

I give students time to share trial drafts during Writing Workshops (see above). Their drafts may range in length from one paragraph to several pages.

ORGANIZING THE ESSAY

I try hard not to sound rigid about organization. My primary goal is to emphasize that structure helps to get ideas across and so students should think through how they organize their work. Following the chart that illustrates a relatively traditional format for an interpretive essay, I include ideas for alternative approaches. Among the student essays that have gone this route are the one in which a student wrote a letter to Shadrach Cohen, objecting to what she considered to be his nondemocratic behavior toward his sons in

"The Americanization of Shadrach Cohen"; a letter from Sigmund Freud to James Joyce analyzing the psychology of "Araby," with material drawn from the student writer's Psychology 101 course; a court drama is which the judge decides whether to give custody of Honoria to Charlie or Marion in "Babylon Revisited"; a letter from Charlie Wales ("Babylon Revisited") to the narrator in "Like a Bad Dream," warning him to act morally lest he suffer Charlie's lonely fate; and a twelve-page "journal" in which a student wrote about her Thai culture and how various stories from other cultures had helped her understand her own background more clearly.

The Introduction

Again, I am trying to offer many possibilities. The introduction is important in orienting the reader and setting the writer on a productive path.

Fulfilling a reader's expectations

In the section titled COMMON FEATURES OF THE INTRODUCTION, I suggest two ways to focus on a particular topic or topics: state a point or raise a question. These are the most commonly used approaches. But I have read successful student essays in which the students do something different.

Drafting an introduction

Some writers like to write the body of the paper before they write the introduction. For a trial draft, any kind of introduction, even no introduction, is acceptable. In writing workshops, students can help each other devise appropriate introductions that reflect the focus of the paper.

Developing a focal point

I resist using the term *thesis* for an introduction because that word suggests to me that the writer is making a claim/proving a point when, in fact, it is just as appropriate to ask or imply a question; furthermore, a thesis may appear only in a conclusion. In my mind, too, the words *focus* and *focal point* are more commonly used in everyday speech and so may give students a less daunting sense of how to approach a literary work. It is easier for most of them to answer the question, "What are you focusing on?" than the question, "What is your thesis?"

What students ultimately do focus on is the culmination of a lengthy process of reading, writing, discussing, and rereading. Many times students select their topics from the literary journal topics and expand on those entries. Other students have to do a lot of writing before the significant ideas come into focus. Some of them cannot articulate a focus until they have a one-on-one conference and explain to me what they are trying to say.

ACTIVITY: Finding evidence to support a focal point. Even in a story as short as "The Story of an Hour," there are many different areas to focus on. Each of the six examples has a slightly different angle. Yet the same or similar details can be used as support.

Providing general background information

This section provides numerous possibilities for opening an introduction. The guideline to go from the general to the specific is not meant to be rigid; there are many ways to start an essay.

A Student Writer at Work

Two versions of Rosa's introduction are included here. I want students to get some sense of the mess and struggle that getting started can entail. Too many students get frustrated if they think they are the only ones who have difficulty.

ACTIVITY: Evaluating introductions. I would like to be able to report here what is good and bad about each of the four sample student introductions. But each time I read them, I have different reactions; and when students have evaluated them, they have said radically different things, positively and negatively. What does this mean? To some extent, an introduction (or any piece of writing) is only as successful as it appears to be to a particular reader at any given moment. That is a humbling thought for instructors, who are burdened with the responsibility of not only evaluating but also grading student writing. [*Note:* Of course, an introduction cannot be evaluated legitimately until it is read in the context of the entire essay. Only then can a reader see if the opening paragraph(s) appropriately reflect(s) what the essay actually does.]

66

ACTIVITY: Examining your own introduction. This "X-Ray" form should be presented with caution since it is valuable to different students at different times and altogether worthless to other students.

The Body

I try in this section to provide some flexibility for students while at the same time emphasizing the importance of structuring their ideas. Again, this section might look rigid (first put this, then put that), but it is designed to provide tools for students who need them. When I present a mini-lesson in organizing, it is usually at the time of an essay assignment. Together the class chooses a sample topic and makes diagrams or lists on the board to show different ways to organize an essay on that topic, much as I have done with "The Story of an Hour" in this section. I emphasize as they do this that there are many options and that they may revise for structure at various stages in the writing process.

A Student Writer at Work

I find that examples of student work are more powerful teaching tools than my instructions. In The International Story, I repeatedly use Rosa's work to show how her ideas developed. In my classes, I also use the work of students in the class to expand the repertoire of examples and because students learn so much from one another.

ACTIVITY: Connecting quotation and interpretation. Students are asked to discuss whether Rosa's interpretations help them understand the quotations she includes. The focus of the discussion is on the content of the piece; but as they look at this sample of writing, they can get a sense of how to incorporate quotations into an essay.

ACTIVITY: Analyzing the body of an essay. If the class has read "The Story of an Hour" and has discussed it at length (for example, in ways suggested in Chapters 1 and 2), then they will be quite familiar with it and able to understand what Rosa does in her essay. Students may come up with ideas that Rosa didn't think of and/or they may disagree with her approach. Such comments make for lively discussion.

Linking individual paragraphs

I like to have students think about paragraphs as linked units rather than as individual entities. The important message is that what is contained in any given paragraph in the body of an essay relates in some way to what came before and what will follow.

ACTIVITY: Analyzing a link between paragraphs. The points in the left-hand margin, written by me, sum up what I perceive Rosa has done in each paragraph. I was able to write that summary only by looking at the whole paragraph, not at any given sentence. What students should look for is whether Rosa moves logically from one paragraph to another. It can be argued that in paragraph 9 Rosa is linking the point that Mrs. Mallard "is going to act in a different way from the way she normally does" to the point made in the previous paragraph that "Mrs. Mallard, being the respectful and good woman that she knows she is, cannot accept these strange feelings that are trying to possess her." In paragraph 8, she has told us what Mrs. Mallard "normally" is: "respectful and good." Of course, students may not see this link readily. Or they may see another link. Or they may see no link at all. If the latter is true, they can add a sentence or phrase to Rosa's paragraph to improve upon it.

ACTIVITY: Organizing the body of an essay. Students should do this activity only when they are ready and only if it is useful.

The Conclusion

The easiest conclusions to write are usually those in which students answer the question(s) they raised in the introduction. It is more difficult for them to know what to say if they already made a point in the introduction. That is one reason why I have offered suggestions for linking the point to a larger meaning of the story. Not all literary analysis is written in this way. But I have found that this approach pushes students toward more in-depth interpretations of what they read. For example, if they only make and prove a point about a character (for example, the character is selfish), then they haven't provided much insight into the story. When they are asked to explore a theme, on the other hand, they need to think about why the author has created a selfish character and what larger significance this might have. Is the author making a general observation about the society in which the story is set?

about human behavior? about ethics/religion/morality/gender/ culture? about the past/present/future?

Although most students will be able to make connections between the story and a larger meaning, a few may remain unable to unravel the mystery that a story contains. For that reason, I accept conclusions that simply raise questions or that offer multiple interpretations.

A Student Writer at Work

Rosa's essay begins with a repetition of the point she made in the introduction. (*Note:* This is only one approach to conclusion writing. Not all writers repeat their points, although most do make some reference to them.) Rosa then links the point (that Louise Mallard is not hard or callous) to a larger meaning (that she is a victim of an oppressive society in which women were viewed as objects of possession).

ACTIVITY: Organizing an essay. I have had some success with helping students organize confusing drafts by using the chart that is printed at the beginning of the section on organizing. In class or in conference, students create three boxes in which they write (1) what they are focusing on, (2) what evidence they are using to elaborate on their ideas, and (3) what larger meaning emerges. In the second box, they also list the supporting points and evidence so that they can see if ideas follow one another logically. If not, they can rearrange the list and revise the paper accordingly. Again, this approach does not work for all students.

WRITING AND EVALUATING AN INTERIM DRAFT

By the time they get to the point of writing a draft that will be read by others, students have done a lot of writing: reading log entries, annotations, class notes, literary journal entries, trial draft, and so on. So they should have quite a bit of material to draw on. The guidelines here are based on the assumption that a lot of thinking has already taken place.

A Student Writer at Work

Although much of Rosa's writing is included in The International Story, there is also much that has not been included. She wrote several drafts and notes, but I felt it would be counterproductive to include them all.

Checklist for Content: Self-Evaluation

The checklist gives students a quick reference to see if they have fulfilled the basic expectations for the draft. I don't grade drafts, so they are never treated as tests of students' ability to follow directions or to fulfill expectations. Rather, they are treated as teaching tools of the course, giving students a chance to examine and organize, and then reexamine and reorganize, their thinking.

RECEIVING FEEDBACK ON A DRAFT

In my course, students receive feedback from me as well as from one another.

Peer Review

Students can be unbelievably helpful to one another, and so I find it productive to take advantage of their class time together to have them read one another's work. But they can also be unintentionally hurtful in their criticisms, and so I find it necessary to have a pretraining session before they become peer reviewers.

ACTIVITY: Discussing guidelines for giving and accepting feedback. I find it best to take a somewhat humorous approach to feedback. The picture of the woman begging for mercy from the judge is worth a thousand words, I think. Students (like instructors) need to think about how they feel when they receive criticism so that they can empathize with those to whom they give it. Likewise, they need to learn strategies for accepting criticism so that the pair or group work does not degenerate into an argument.

The Peer Review Form can be xeroxed and handed out to students to act as a guideline to remind them of psychologically sound ways of giving criticism. They may give oral or written responses to one another's work, depending on which is deemed more effective or useful. The box titled Guidelines for Peer Reviewing suggests ways to engage students in pair or small-group work. Alternatively, I have a few students present their drafts to the whole class (this process is followed several times during the semester for different essay assignments, until each student has the opportunity to participate). The students mimeograph enough copies of the paper for each member of the class (or for class members to share comfortably), read the draft aloud, and discuss their ideas with the class.

ACTIVITY: Peer reviewing. Whether students work in pairs or small groups or as a whole class, they can use the guidelines in this activity to shape their discussion. But these suggestions are just that: suggestions. Students may find it useful simply to discuss the content of their respective papers. In the process of discussing ideas, they usually get feedback on weak areas and know instinctively that they should make revisions for clarity. Furthermore, as they discuss what a story may mean, they discover more ideas to write about.

Instructor's Comments

For years, I wrote detailed comments in the margins and at the end of students' papers. Then one year, a student pointed out that I had written more than she had. I think she might have been telling me that she appreciated the time and effort I had put in, but I started to think that there was something wrong with what I was doing. Wasn't the idea to have the students, not the instructor, do the writing?

Now, instead of taking so much time responding to early drafts with lengthy written comments, I read them and make brief comments, which are actually notes to myself to tell me what I want to cover in a one-on-one conference. Then, having cut down significantly on the responding-in-writing time, I meet with each student individually.

I begin the conference with the statement, "Tell me about the process you went through to write this draft." I then sit back and listen to what is often a revealing tale. In describing what they have done, many students actually reveal what they _intended_ to do, not what they accomplished. They then realize that the paper may not reflect what they want it to, and we discuss how they can revise the paper to reflect their intentions. I keep a pen and legal-size notepad on my desk so that students can write down what they want to add to or change in their drafts. I feel a conference has been successful if a student does most of the talking and leaves with a sheet full of self-generated ideas. Of course, I do speak in the conference, usually to ask questions, to answer the student's questions about the story, and/or to share my initial reactions to what the student wrote. I give direct advice when I think it is appropriate. Some students, for personal or cultural reasons, need direct instructional intervention in order to learn how to proceed.

Note: I do write comments on students' final papers.

REVISING

The guidelines for revising are designed to help students see the large picture. Revising does not mean just correcting errors.

A Student Writer at Work

The instructor's comment that is included here is an excerpt from the lengthy comments I wrote on Rosa's paper a few years ago. As I mentioned earlier, these days I am more likely to give primarily oral responses, in class and in conference; and the advice is less directive, with my comments aimed at getting the student to discover what kind of revision is necessary or could be meaningful. It is not that I think direct advice is bad; it is just that I have found that most students can give themselves good advice, under my guidance. And I think that that will help them more in the long run: ultimately they will have to edit their own work without my help.

The peer reviewer's comment that is included here was given orally. Students typically give each other positive reinforcement and then ask questions of one another.

COMPLETING THE ESSAY

Given that students have access to word processors on campus, I encourage them to type their papers. To help students who do not know how to use a word processor, I arrange group instruction with a staff member at the computer center.

STUDENT ESSAY

I recognize that Rosa has not written the "perfect" essay; none of my students ever has. But I was impressed with the depth of her analysis and think it is a useful model for students.

CHAPTER 6: Selecting Evidence for Critical Analysis of a Story

There is no way that all of the material in this chapter can be absorbed by students before they begin to write their first interpretive essay. Throughout the semester, little by little, through reading/writing/discussing, students become more knowledgeable about the contents of Chapter 6.

By the time they are ready to write an essay, students already have written reading log and literary journal entries and discussed those entries in class. The entries have served as the springboard for further discussion about the fictional elements and abstract ideas in the stories. Therefore, without much in the way of traditional teacher-dominated lessons about literature, students have discovered key ways to get at a story's meanings.

For the first essay assignment, I emphasize primarily the sections in Chapter 6 on character, setting, and abstract ideas. I find that these are the areas that most students concentrate on when they write essays. I try to make the material in Chapter 6 a natural part of the class discussions. I usually put reading assignments on the syllabus that include these sections and advise students to use them for reference as they prepare their essays.

I will first explain the sections in general and then explain specific activities section by section.

Analyzing Key Words and Phrases

Since this kind of analysis happens in class, these particular excerpts do not need to be focused on out of context. Students who refer to these sections when they work on their papers should recognize that they have already done this kind of analysis in reading log and/or journal entries and in class discussions. Reading over these sections can be especially helpful to students who do not apply readily what they do for class to what they are expected to do in an essay.

Developing a Vocabulary

Students often complain about not having a sophisticated enough vocabulary with which to discuss a story. Many students appreciate having lists of words to refer to when they are composing. Some of these activities ask students to use the dictionary to discover subtle differences of meaning in words that are listed as synonyms. If there is time, this can be a useful activity for the whole class to engage in. If not, the list can act as a resource for individual students who have difficulty expressing themselves precisely.

Students sometimes are asked to create a scene that fits the definition of a word (for example, in the section on character, they can select a word such as "successful" or "passive" and then describe a circumstance in which this character trait is revealed). These activities can be oral or written. If successful, the activity can give students insight into how ideas emerge from details.

Asking Questions

The list of questions is not meant to be exhaustive or applicable to all stories.

Focusing on a Topic

This section is designed to give students some idea of the kinds of topics that might be appropriate for an interpretive essay. The list of topics is not meant to be exhaustive or applicable to all stories.

CHARACTER

I sometimes ask questions such as, "What would you have done (and why) if he/she/they were your roommate/spouse/friends?" and "What would you have done (and why) in his/her/their place?" When students talk about the characters as though their situations could be real, they seem to have little trouble analyzing them. I also try to have them look at the characters from different perspectives: for example, a character from the perspective of someone of the same gender and someone of the opposite gender; a Chinese character from the perspective of a Chinese and a non-Chinese; and so on. This approach often makes students question their own interpretations.

ACTIVITY: Analyzing key words and phrases related to character. This activity asks students to analyze the husband's character in the first paragraph of Mishima's story, "Swaddling Clothes." Students may observe that the husband is an actor, that he is "attractive," that he's too "busy" to spend time with his wife, that he's callous and unsympathetic toward her fear of returning home. They may guess that the "Western-style" furniture was his choice, as Toshiko finds it "unhomely." This difference in taste suggests that his Western values may be in conflict with his wife's (traditional Japanese) values.

ACTIVITY: Identifying character traits. This activity is designed to encourage students to capture succinctly the essence of a given character. Different students may come up with different yet appropriate adjectives to describe Toshiko, depending on their background, culture, and/or the details they focus on: "submissive," "kind," "foolish," "depressed," and so on.

SETTING

The example in this section is taken from a story that is not reprinted in The International Story, Joyce Carol Oates's "Where Are You Going, Where Have You Been?" I did not want to use only stories that are reprinted in the book lest I do too much analysis that students could be doing on their own. I have italicized different clues at two different times to give students an understanding of how they might sweep back over a story and focus on new details that reveal new interpretations.

ACTIVITY: Analyzing key words and phrases related to setting. Among the discoveries that students might make about this paragraph is that the key elements of the setting are "the mosque, the river, and the fields," which the narrator describes as "the landmarks of our life." The river and the fields represent the outdoors, the natural scene where the narrator spent his happy childhood. The mosque, where the narrator studied the Koran, was associated with "love"; the boy obviously has a positive attitude toward his religion. Overall, the setting reflects joy.

After students have finished this story, it is interesting for them to go back to look at the first paragraph. They can be encouraged to focus on the *Chapter of the Merciful* that the narrator remembers reciting. Although the detail may have been overlooked the first time, now students may recognize the irony of the merciless grandfather's pride at his grandson's recitation.

POINT OF VIEW

In this section I use as an example the opening of John Updike's "A&P." Usually students find this to be a humorous piece but some students who are not familiar with certain features of American adolescent culture may be confused or even offended. Because this paragraph is full of idioms that may be unfamiliar to nonnative speakers of English, it may need extra explanation. One reason I am partial to this paragraph is because of Updike's use of grammar. While I never teach literature for the purpose of teaching grammar, I believe that grammar is a good tool for interpreting literature. In this example, which begins "In walks these three girls," the reader is immediately confronted with a so-called nonstandard version of English. The class can guess/discuss why this is done.

This paragraph is also useful for discussing the concept of reliability. What makes a person (narrator) reliable or unreliable? age? gender? education? values? The answer to these questions depends on the relationship between narrator and reader as well as on other factors.

ACTIVITY: Analyzing key words and phrases related to point of view. Among the things that students might notice is that the story has a first-person narrator who is a character in the story. They may be struck by the fact that the narrator lived on "Sadness Street," perhaps a hint of family problems. The fact that the driver speaks to the narrator "slowly and with funny gestures" and that the narrator challenges the driver by pointing out that he is "not a foreigner" but "a Persian just like yourself" holds a number of clues. First, the setting (Iran) is established when it becomes clear that both driver and passenger are Persian (Iranian). But, more significantly perhaps, we also become aware that the narrator may not sound Persian; for some reason, he appears to be a foreigner. Students who have had the experience of studying outside their native countries and then returning to their home countries may immediately recognize what is going on here. Many of them become Americanized, even without realizing it, and do not appear to be native speakers when they first arrive back home. They will identify with the narrator's dual cultural perspective.

ACTIVITY: Analyzing point of view. This activity, which can be oral or written, can give students practice in using the present tense to describe what an author is doing in a work of fiction. Again, such an exercise can be done with many stories. And it need not be a separate exercise but can be integrated naturally into a class discussion of a story.

IMAGERY

It can be effective to read aloud the sentences taken from Ray Bradbury's "There Will Come Soft Rains." Once students know that the story is about a nuclear attack, they can form mental images as they hear lines such as "The house stood alone in a city of rubble and ashes."

In analyzing the beginning of the third paragraph of James Joyce's "Araby," I try to show how a reader can take an analytical approach toward imagery. For example, I provide the primary dictionary meaning of the word *dark* ("with little or no light") and then provide other definitions that give a negative connotation to the scene ("gloomy," "evil," "threatening," "unenlightened"). To answer the question, "What might Joyce be suggesting by using the word *dark?*" students might go through these definitions one by one (as well as others) and see how the interpretation of the scene changes with each meaning. Joyce might be commenting on the lack of optimism (gloom), the danger (evil), the potential harm (threatening), and/or the lack of spiritual understanding/insight (unenlightened) of the society in which the boys are growing up. By combining negative and positive images ("muddy lanes," "dripping gardens," "odorous stables"), Joyce could be implying that things are not what they appear to be or sound like. The physical landmarks of the neighborhood (lanes, gardens, stables) sound lovely, but there may be something ominous about them (muddy, dripping, odorous). By the time the story is finished, we learn that the boy is disillusioned by his experiences. It may be that in looking back on his childhood, the adult narrator recognizes that as a child he was blind to reality, feeling only the joy of youthful play without yet knowing the limitations of life in Dublin.

ACTIVITY: Analyzing images. Among the images that students might focus on are those related to Belayeff's appearance: he's "rosy" and "well fed." From these details, students may imagine a man who is physically a bit heavy. They may also assume that he is not poor, not only because he eats well but also because he is a "gentleman." Depending on their own values vis-a-vis racetrack betting, they may question Belayeff's values, for he is "a patron of the race-tracks." Although he is described as "young," his actual age is given as "thirty-two," which to some students may sound old; different readers will imagine a different person. Perhaps the most significant image is the metaphor of Belayeff's romance with Olga, which is described as a book whose "first thrilling, inspiring pages" have turned into a story that "was now dragging wearily on." Such an image, combined with other images, may give some readers a negative impression of Belayeff: a man who has nothing better to do than to go to the racetracks and make love to a woman he does not even care about. Other readers may feel sorry for him or find him amusing. It can be interesting for students to go back to the first paragraph after they have finished the story, to test their first impression against their final impression of Belayeff.

ACTIVITY: Writing about images. This activity may be useful for students who have trouble analyzing images, but it should be used with caution to avoid tedium.

SYMBOLISM

There can be a fine line between imagery and symbolism. (It might be wise to emphasize that a symbol is an object/event meant to stand for something else rather than just to suggest something else.) When teaching international literature, it can be even more difficult to draw the line because words/images do not necessarily have the same meanings or connotations in one culture that they do in another. Teaching groups of students from different cultures further complicates the process because what is a symbol in one culture may not be in another. Such discussions greatly enrich the classroom.

To illustrate symbolic use of language, I analyze the first paragraph of James Joyce's "Araby." The word blind is stated twice, giving it special emphasis. I have included the American Heritage Dictionary's thirteen definitions of blind. (Just looking at the dictionary definition should make instructors aware of how difficult it can be to look words up in a dictionary for the purpose of understanding the reading, especially for a nonnative speaker of English.) In searching for symbols, the first step is to find the literal meaning. Here, a "blind end" is a dead-end street. (Note: blind end is the common term in Great Britain for the U.S. term dead end.) After more symbolic meanings of the word are discussed, I ask the question, "What might the blind street symbolize?" Students may answer that since the boys are "set . . . free" into a street that has no exit, no way out, Joyce may be implying that there is no future for them in Dublin, no possibility for advancement. Or that they may be blind to reality, thinking that they are set free when in fact they are trapped. And so on.

ACTIVITY: Analyzing key words and phrases to discover symbolism. Here the chicken takes center stage. Students may see the chicken as a symbol of a human being or the chicken/egg cycle as a symbol of the life cycle in general. At first the chicken looks precious ("tiny fluffy"), full of possibilities, just like a much-wanted newborn baby. But the cycle is "dreadful" because the chicken grows up ("becomes hideously naked"), gets sick and dies. Only a few chickens survive to maturity and those survivors give birth to more chickens who get sick and die. Life is complex. If students have read the whole story, they may interpret the passage in other ways. For example, they may see the cycle of birth/death as symbolic of happiness/tragedy, the American dream/ disillusionment, or success/failure.

TONE

Tone is an important concept to explain, as it taps into not merely students' reactions to a story but what they think the author thinks. It's not easy (and not always necessary) to get at what an author may think, but analyzing tone is one way to get there. To move students toward articulating the tone of a story, I often ask them, "Do you like (this character)? Why or why not? What is there in this story--for example, words, actions--that makes you like or dislike the character?" or "How do you feel about what happens? Why? What is there in this story--for example, conversations, events--that makes you feel this way?" If students can identify their own reactions first, they may be able go back to the story to discover why they feel as they do. Often (not always, of course), they feel a certain way because the author has used certain words to manipulate feelings and attitudes.

ACTIVITY: Analyzing diction and sentence development. This activity asks students to analyze the opening lines of Xi Xi's "A Woman Like Me." Some of the significant adjectives ("unsuitable," "emotional," "cruel," "powerless," "innocent," "hidden," "unhappy") and/or nouns ("blame," "trap," "escape," "Fate," "trick," "fault") might make students feel sad or depressed. Three sentences are relatively short: "A woman like me is actually unsuitable for any man's love"; "I am totally powerless to resist Fate"; "That's exactly how I feel about him." The rest are quite long, ranging in length from twenty to forty-seven words. Why this is so students can only speculate. Students should think about the circumstances in which they use a lot of words to express themselves. Perhaps, for example, the character's lengthy sentences reflect a need to defend herself, and for some reason the explanations do not come easily.

It is difficult for students to determine the author's attitude toward the narrator. As with all literary works, many interpretations are possible. Based on the line, "I am totally powerless to resist Fate," some students say that the author is critical of the narrator's passivity. Others say that the author feels sorry for her because she is trapped.

ABSTRACT IDEA

Analyzing elements of fiction (*character, setting,* and so on) is a traditional way of interpreting literature, but it is far from the only way. This section suggests that students can begin with an idea or issue and trace it throughout a story. This approach opens up the possibility for students to write more personal essays. For example, students might want to compare their own experiences growing up with the experiences of a character in a story or of characters in several stories. Or they might want to write more argumentative essays, for example, editorials in which they voice their opinion on a subject such as racism or war, while drawing from one or more stories. Or they might want to write more ideological essays. For example, they can examine a story or group of stories from a feminist, cultural, or psychoanalytic perspective.

The example I analyze is Kate Chopin's "The Story of an Hour." While I focus on the subject of freedom, there are many other issues that students could focus on in this story, for example, marriage, a woman's role in society, death.

CHAPTER 7: Quoting and Documenting Sources

Many students need help to learn why, when, and how to quote and document. Although there are rules for these conventions, decisions about quoting and documenting often are individualistic, depending on a writer's purpose and style. My aim is to help students develop a sense of when and how quoting and documenting sources are appropriate for their particular essays.

It takes a long time for some students to develop this sense, especially if much of their schooling took place outside the United States. For example, writing from sources in some countries may mean copying text without using quotation marks; the teacher is always familiar with the source and the student is expected to reproduce it verbatim.

QUOTING

The literary journal project gives students the opportunity to practice selecting and incorporating quotations over time and in relatively nonjudgmental circumstances. Although I do not correct many grammatical errors in the journals--I respond to ideas--I do make a point of showing students how to improve upon their quoting technique: ways to introduce, comment on, punctuate quotations, etc. At the beginning of the term, for example, I might pull out some sentences from the journal entries that contain poorly framed quotations, put them on the board, and have students reshape the sentences. Later, I pull out passages from student essays that use quotations improperly, type the passages onto a handout, and have the class decide various ways to incorporate the quotations effectively. I also underline improperly framed quotations in students' papers so that students can self correct. I sometimes refer students to the appropriate page number in The International Story to find the rule for punctuating a quotation.

ACTIVITY: Selecting a quotation. This activity asks students to find quotations that can support each statement. Here are possible answers:
1.   ". . . the face that had never looked save with love upon her."
2.   "What could love, the unsolved mystery, count for in face of this possession of self-assertion which she suddenly recognized as the strongest impulse of her being!"
3.   "When the storm of grief had spent itself she went away to her room alone. She would have no one follow her."
4.   "Josephine was kneeling before the closed door . . . . "
5.   "The delicious breath of rain was in the air."
6.   "She was young, with a fair, calm face, whose lines bespoke repression and even a certain strength."

ACTIVITY: Integrating quotations. This activity asks students to select a quotation from a story and incorporate it into a sample student paragraph. Here are possible answers:
1.   For instance, they are symbolized in the image of "patches of blue sky showing here and there through the clouds that had . . . piled one above the other," where the clouds stand for sorrow and despair and the sky symbolizes the advent of a

happier life . . . . Chopin provides two hints for this conclusion: the first, more obvious implication is given in the term, "new spring life." . . . . The second, more subtle hint is symbolized in the haunting image of the woman sinking into a "comfortable, roomy armchair." . . . . Our imagination is even supported by Chopin, who compares Louise to a child who "had cried itself to sleep [and] continues to sob in its dreams."

2.   At the beginning of the story, we are told that Mrs. Mallard is "afflicted with a heart trouble." . . . . We view her exaggerated grief at the opening of the story, when she immediately cries uncontrollably at the news of her husband's death: "She wept at once, with sudden wild abandonment." . . . . . But Mrs. Mallard doesn't question the news: "She did not hear the story as many women have heard the same, with a paralyzed inability to accept its significance."

CITING AND DOCUMENTING SOURCES

Most of the documenting students do is connected to course material, that is, to the stories in The International Story. But sometimes students refer to outside sources and need to know how to document that material properly.

If a student is having difficulty paraphrasing text, during writing workshops or in one-on-one conferences I read a passage aloud, ask the student to repeat orally (in the student's own words) what it says, have the student put the explanation in writing (if it is accurate), and then say, "That's a paraphrase!"

ACTIVITY: Paraphrasing and quoting to avoid plagiarism. This activity asks students (1) to paraphrase a passage and (2) to write a sentence in which they quote from the passage. Here are possible responses:

1.   In her article, "The Context of The Awakening," Margaret Culley points out that even though there were social and political improvements in the 1890s, women continued to face obstacles in many areas, and most people felt that a woman's obligation was to be a perfect homemaker.

2.   Margaret Culley emphasizes that women's freedom was limited in the 1890s and that most people thought it was a woman's "sacred duty" to be at home (119).

CHAPTER 8: The Editing Process

This chapter gives students some guidelines for proofreading and editing their writing, emphasizing that they should check to see that they have followed certain conventions of writing about literature.

ADDRESSING ERROR

I expect error; it is natural and inevitable. Slowly, over time, with practice and guidance, students internalize an increasing number of grammatical and syntactical structures, many of which come from their reading. I do not expect miracles in one semester.

I simply underline error, or I help students locate error during a student-teacher conference. I give students time to correct their own work and to consult with me or someone else for those errors that they cannot correct on their own. I sometimes hand back papers with errors underlined and give the whole class time to correct as many of their own and each others' errors as they can. I then move around the room to help individual students with problem areas. Many of these issues are resolved by discussing what students mean rather than what grammar rule they missed. I ask for clarification if students' word choices or garbled syntax result in sentences that simply do not seem to make sense. Usually, I ask students to explain their ideas and then to write down what they just said; or to rewrite a sentence in two or three other ways.

One exception to this teacher-underlines/student-corrects guideline is vocabulary. Rather than underlining an inappropriate or unsophisticated word or phrase, I help to expand vocabulary by providing a more appropriate or sophisticated word or by supplying a list of possible alternatives.

GRADING STUDENT WRITING

I rarely grade individual papers. I agree with Peter Elbow, who argues that ranking individual papers is arbitrary and uninformative (see College English, February 1993, 187-206). I express judgment of final papers by commenting in writing on strengths and weaknesses, without having to justify a grade. At the end of the semester, I grade the body of the students' work, which they have collected in a portfolio. The final course grade, then, reflects what the student has accomplished over time rather than only what the student has failed to do at any given moment.

SAMPLE COURSE PLAN

The following plan shows how one could use all of the stories in The International Story, in chronological order in this case, in a course that meets for fifteen weeks.

Week   1
Introduction to the course
Week   2
"The Necklace" / "A Trifle from Real Life"
Week   3
"Two Portraits" / "The Americanization of Shadrach Cohen"
Week   4
Writing Workshop / **First Essay Due**
Week   5
"Araby" / "War"
Week   6
"The Egg" / "Babylon Revisited" / **Revision Due**
Week   7
"The Man Who Was Almost a Man" / Writing Workshop
Week   8
Second Essay Due / "Dead Men's Path"
and/or "Six Feet of the Country"
Week   9
"Like a Bad Dream" / "Swaddling Clothes" / **Revision   Due**
Week   10
"A Handful of Dates" and/or "The Plane Reservation" /
Writing Workshop
Week   11
Third Essay Due / Workshop on Final Project
Week   12
"The Verb *to Kill*" / "Girl" / "A Woman Like Me"
Week   13
"The Street-Sweeping Show" and/or "The Grass-Eaters" /
Revision Due /
"Las papas" and/or "Village"
Week   14
Writing Workshop / **Fourth Essay Due**
Week   15
Final (Novel, Poetry, or Research) Project Due
End of semester:
   Optional: Revision of Fourth Essay

THEMATIC ARRANGEMENT OF STORIES

Childhood and Adolescence

"Araby," "The Egg," "Girl," "A Handful of Dates," "The Man Who Was Almost a Man," "A Trifle from Real Life," "Two Portraits," "The Verb *to Kill*"

Parents and Children

"The Americanization of Shadrach Cohen," "Babylon Revisited," "The Egg," "Girl," "A Handful of Dates," "The Man Who Was Almost a Man," "Las papas," "The Plane Reservation," "A Trifle from Real Life", "Swaddling Clothes," "Two Portraits," "War"

Love and Marriage / Women and Men

"The Egg," "The Grass-Eaters," "Like a Bad Dream," "The Necklace," "The Plane Reservation," "Six Feet of the Country," "The Story of an Hour," "Swaddling Clothes," "A Trifle from Real Life," "Two Portraits," "A Woman Like Me"

Work

"The Americanization of Shadrach Cohen," "Babylon Revisited," "Dead Men's Path," "The Egg," "The Grass-Eaters," "A Handful of Dates," "Like a Bad Dream," "The Man Who Was Almost a Man," "The Necklace," "The Street-Sweeping Show," "A Woman Like Me"

Cultural Identity

"The Americanization of Shadrach Cohen," "Dead Men's Path," "Las papas," "The Plane Reservation," "Six Feet of the Country," "Swaddling Clothes," "Village"

Religious, Ethical, and Sociopolitical Issues

"The Americanization of Shadrach Cohen," "Araby," "Dead Men's Path," "The Grass-Eaters," "A Handful of Dates," "Like a Bad Dream," "Six Feet of the Country," "The Story of an Hour," "The Street-Sweeping Show," "Swaddling Clothes," "Two Portraits," "The Verb *to Kill*," "Village," "War," "A Woman Like Me"

85

SHORT STORIES: SELECTED BIBLIOGRAPHY

International Literature

Achebe, Chinua, and C. L. Innes, eds. The Heinemann Book of Contemporary African Short Stories. London: Heinemann, 1992.

Agosin, Marjorie, ed. Landscapes of a New Land: Short Fiction by Latin American Women. New York: White Pine, 1989.

Carver, Ann C., and Sung-Sheng Yvonne Chang, eds. Bamboo Shoots after the Rain: Contemporary Stories by Women Writers of Taiwan. New York: Feminist, 1990.

Esteves, Carmen C., and Lizabeth Paravisini-Gebert, eds. Green Cane and Juicy Flotsam: Short Stories by Caribbean Women. New Brunswick: Rutgers U P, 1991.

Fadiman, Clifton, ed. The World of the Short Story: A 20th Century Collection. Boston: Houghton, 1986.

Halpern, Daniel, ed. The Art of the Tale: An International Anthology of Short Stories. New York: Penguin, 1988.

Hamalian, Leo, and John D. Yohannan, eds. New Writing from the Middle East: Arabic, Armenian, Israeli, Persian, Turkish Literatures. New York: Ungar, 1978.

Holmstrom, Lakshimi, ed. The Inner Courtyard: Stories by Indian Women. London: Virago, 1990.

Howe, Irving, and Ilana Weiner Howe, eds. Short Shorts: An Anthology of the Shortest Stories. Toronto: Bantam, 1983.

Johnson-Davies, Denys, trans. and ed. Arabic Short Stories. London: Quartet, 1983.

Lee, Peter H., ed. Flowers of Fire: Twentieth-Century Korean Stories. Honolulu: U of Hawaii P, 1986.

Ondaatje, Michael, ed. From Ink Lake: Canadian Stories. New York: Viking, 1990.

Santos, Rosario, ed. And We Sold the Rain: Contemporary Fiction from Central America. New York: Four Walls Eight Windows, 1988.

Shapard, Robert, and James Thomas, eds. Sudden Fiction International: 60 Short-Short Stories. New York: Norton, 1989.

Solomon, Barbara H., ed. Other Voices, Other Vistas: Short Stories from Africa, China, India, Japan, and Latin America. New York: Penguin, 1992.

Tai, Jeanne, trans. and ed. Spring Bamboo: A Collection of Contemporary Chinese Short Stories. New York: Random, 1989.

Allen, Paula Gunn. Spider Woman's Granddaughters: Traditional Tales and Contemporary Writing of Native American Women. New York: Ballantine, 1989.

Antler, Joyce, ed. America and I: Short Stories by American Jewish Women Writers. Boston: Beacon, 1990.

Brown, Wesley, and Amy Ling, eds. Imagining America: Stories from the Promised Land. New York: Persea, 1991.

Lim, Shirley Geok-Lin, Mayumi Tsutakawa, and Margaret Donnelly, eds. Forbidden Stitch: An Asian American Women's Anthology. Corvallis, CO: Calyx, 1989.

McMillan, Terry, ed. Breaking Ice: An Anthology of Contemporary African-American Fiction. New York: Penguin, 1990.

Ortiz, Simon, ed. Earth Power Coming: Short Fiction in Native American Literature. Tsaile, AZ: Navajo, 1983.

Poey, Delia, and Virgil Suarez, eds. Iguana Dreams: New Latino Fiction. New York: HarperCollins, 1992.

Simmen, Edward, ed. North of the Rio Grande: The Mexican- American Experience in Short Fiction. New York: Penguin, 1992.

Reference   Tools

I n d e x
  Short Story Index.
Biography
  Contemporary Authors.
  Current Biography Yearbook.
C r i t i c i s m
  Twentieth-Century Short Story Explication.
  MLA Bibliography.
  American Short Fiction Criticism and Scholarship 1959-1977.
F i l m
  The American Short Story video series. Available from Perspective Films, 65 East South Water St., Chicago, IL 60601. Companion anthologies edited by Calvin Skaggs (Dell 1977/1980).

  Emmens, Carol A. Short Stories on Film and Video. Littleton, CO: Libraries Unlimited, 1985.

  Wheeler, David, ed. No, but I Saw the Movie: The Best Short Stories Ever Made into Film. New York: Penguin, 1989.

TEACHING LITERATURE: SELECTED BIBLIOGRAPHY

Beach, Richard. A Teacher's Introduction to Reader-Response Theories. Urbana, IL: NCTE, 1993.

Biddle, Arthur W., and Toby Fulwiler. Reading, Writing, and the Study of Literature. New York: Random, 1989.

Bogdan, Deanne, and Stanley B. Straw, eds. Beyond Communication: Reading Comprehension and Criticism. Portsmouth, NH: Boynton/Cook, Heinemann, 1990.

Cahalan, James M., and David B. Downing. Practicing Theory in Introductory College Literature Courses. Urbana, IL: NCTE, 1991.

Carter, Ronald, and Michael N. Long. Teaching Literature. New York: Longman, 1991.

Collie, Joanne, and Stephen Slater. Literature in the Language Classroom: A Resource Book of Ideas and Activities. Cambridge: Cambridge U P, 1987.

Eagleton, Terry. Literary Theory: An Introduction. Minneapolis: U of Minnesota P, 1983.

Farrell, Edmund J., and James R. Squire. Transactions with Literature: A Fifty-Year Perspective. Urbana, IL: NCTE, 1990.

Herrington, Anne J. "Teaching, Writing, and Learning: A Naturalistic Study of Writing in an Undergraduate Literature Course." Advances in Writing Research, Volume Two: Writing in Academic Disciplines. Ed. David A. Jolliffe. Norwood, NJ: Ablex, 1988. 133-66.

Langer, Judith A., ed. Literature Instruction: A Focus on Student Response. Urbana, IL: NCTE, 1992.

Nelms, Ben F., ed. Literature in the Classroom: Readers, Texts, and Contexts. Urbana, IL: NCTE, 1988.

Pugh, Sharon L. "Literature, Culture, and ESL: A Natural Convergence." Journal of Reading 32 (1989): 320-29.

Rosenblatt, Louise. Literature as Exploration. 4th ed. New York: MLA, 1983.

Sasser, Linda. "Teaching Literature to Language Minority Students." The Multicultural Classroom: Readings for Content-Area Teachers. Ed. Patricia A. Richard-Amato and Marguerite Ann Snow. New York: Longman, 1992. 300-15.

Spack, Ruth. "Literature, Reading, Writing, and ESL: Bridging the Gaps." TESOL Quarterly 19 (1985): 703-25.

Trimmer, Joseph, and Tilly Warnock, eds. Understanding Others: Cultural and Cross-Cultural Studies and the Teaching of Literature. Urbana, IL: NCTE, 1992.

For EU product safety concerns, contact us at Calle de José Abascal, 56–1°,
28003 Madrid, Spain or eugpsr@cambridge.org.